Guidelines

VOL 28 / PART 3
September–December 2012

Commissioned by **Jeremy Duff;** *edited by* **Lisa Cherrett**

Guidelines © BRF 2012
The Bible Reading Fellowship
15 The Chambers, Vineyard, Abingdon OX14 3FE
Tel: 01865 319700; Fax: 01865 319701
E-mail: enquiries@brf.org.uk; Website: www.brf.org.uk

ISBN 978 1 84101 675 7

Distributed in Australia by Mediacom Education Inc., PO Box 610, Unley, SA 5061.
Tel: 1800 811 311; Fax: 08 8297 8719;
E-mail: admin@mediacom.org.au
Available also from all good Christian bookshops in Australia.
For individual and group subscriptions in Australia:
Mrs Rosemary Morrall, PO Box W35, Wanniassa, ACT 2903.

Distributed in New Zealand by Scripture Union Wholesale, PO Box 760, Wellington
Tel: 04 385 0421; Fax: 04 384 3990; E-mail: suwholesale@clear.net.nz

Publications distributed to more than 60 countries

Printed in Singapore by Craft Print International Ltd

Suggestions for using *Guidelines*

Set aside a regular time and place, if possible, when you can read and pray undisturbed. Before you begin, take time to be still and, if you find it helpful, use the BRF prayer.

In *Guidelines*, the introductory section provides context for the passages or themes to be studied, while the units of comment can be used daily, weekly, or whatever best fits your timetable. You will need a Bible (more than one if you want to compare different translations) as Bible passages are not included. At the end of each week is a 'Guidelines' section, offering further thoughts about, or practical application of what you have been studying.

You may find it helpful to keep a journal to record your thoughts about your study, or to note items for prayer. Another way of using *Guidelines* is to meet with others to discuss the material, either regularly or occasionally.

Occasionally, you may read something in *Guidelines* that you find particularly challenging, even uncomfortable. This is inevitable in a series of notes which draws on a wide spectrum of contributors, and doesn't believe in ducking difficult issues. Indeed, we believe that *Guidelines* readers much prefer thought-provoking material to a bland diet that only confirms what they already think.

If you do disagree with a contributor, you may find it helpful to go through these three steps. First, think about why you feel uncomfortable. Perhaps this is an idea that is new to you, or you are not happy at the way something has been expressed. Or there may be something more substantial—you may feel that the writer is guilty of sweeping generalisation, factual error, theological or ethical misjudgment. Second, pray that God would use this disagreement to teach you more about his word and about yourself. Third, think about what you will do as a result of the disagreement. You might resolve to find out more about the issue, or write to the contributor or the editors of *Guidelines*. After all, we aim to be 'doers of the word', not just people who hold opinions about it.

Writers in this issue

Tim Blewett has been the Warden of Launde Abbey since 2004 and Spirituality Adviser to the Bishop of Leicester since 2010. Previously he was Canon Residentiary of St Asaph Cathedral. He was mobilised by the Army to serve as a military chaplain in Iraq from December 2003 to June 2004, having previously served as a military chaplain in Bosnia in 1997 to 1998.

Andrew Angel lectures at St John's College, Nottingham and is an Anglican priest. In addition to parish ministry, he has taught in secondary schools and higher education. He has published articles in theological journals and written *Chaos and the Son of Man* (LSTS 60; T&T Clark, 2006). Andrew is married to Carol Fabiola and they have two sons.

Jeremy Duff is a vicar in Widnes with a teaching and writing ministry, which has included posts at Liverpool Cathedral and within Oxford University. His writings include *Meeting Jesus: Human Responses to a Yearning God* (SPCK, 2006) and *The Elements of New Testament Greek* (CUP, 2005).

Graham Tomlin is Dean of St Mellitus College, based in London and Chelmsford. He taught theology in Oxford University for many years and is the author of several books, including *The Provocative Church* (SPCK, 2002) and, most recently, *The Prodigal Spirit* (Alpha International, 2011).

Henry Wansbrough OSB is a monk at Ampleforth Abbey in Yorkshire. He is Executive Secretary of the International Commission for Producing an English-Language Lectionary (ICPEL) for the Roman Catholic Church, and lectures frequently across the globe.

Jill Duff is currently working on a research project for the Diocese of Liverpool on what encourages young people to consider ordination in the Church of England. Previously she has been a pioneer minister in Liverpool City Centre and in parish ministry in a deprived part of Liverpool.

Matthew Firth read Natural Sciences at Cambridge and Theology at Oxford. He is chaplain to the Carlisle campuses of the University of Cumbria and is also a pioneer minister for the planting of a new church aimed at people in the 18–30 age-group. He has a particular interest in bringing the Hebrew scriptures to life in today's context.

Jenny Hellyer is a spiritual director, musician, clergy wife and mother based in Oxford. After teaching and theological study, she was part of the Lee Abbey Community in Devon for seven years.

The Editors write…

'A personal God' is a phrase some Christians often use to capture the sense that God is not just a 'force'—a distant omnipotent being—but someone they relate to as individuals. It speaks of God's love, compassion and care for them.

Many of our readings in this edition bring out aspects of this idea of God encountered as 'person'. We start with 'Retreat to focus on God', in which Tim Blewett encourages us to deepen our relationship with God. Then Andrew Angel continues his studies in Mark's Gospel, in which we are pressed to grasp both who Jesus really is and 'the heart of God' seen in his desire to bring salvation. Then Jeremy Duff tackles the Song of Songs, a text whose place in the Bible encourages us to use human experience of love as a pointer to our relationship to God. Juxtaposed with this, we find the cross. Here Graham Tomlin helps us engage with this most stark aspect of Christian belief—suffering and death mixed with love and sacrifice in a brew that is nothing if not emotional and personal.

Next comes our regular foray into the Psalms with Henry Wansbrough, this time with psalms expressing much about what God is really like. After this, Jill Duff, a pioneer minister in Liverpool, gives her 'Reflections of a pioneer'. This is part of our continued commitment to engaging with mission. It also fits with our theme, for it begins and ends with the idea of God's compassion and speaks of how we can be sustained through our closeness to God. Deuteronomy 11—22 follows, where Matthew Firth helps us ponder what it means to be 'the people of God'. If this is what God is like, what does that mean for those who claim to be his people? Finally Jenny Hellyer gives us much to reflect upon at Christmas—the moment when God indeed 'came to us', shockingly taking on human nature, to speak to us person to person.

Lisa Cherrett writes:
With this issue we say 'goodbye' and a very big 'thank you' to the Revd Dr Jeremy Duff as Commissioning Editor of *Guidelines*. Jeremy has been engaged in this role since 2004, and we have appreciated his commitment and vision in steering *Guidelines* through several changes over those years. We hope that he will continue to write for the notes. From the May 2013 issue on, *Guidelines* will be commissioned by the Revd Dr David Spriggs, of Bible Society, who will be familiar to many readers as a contributor in earlier issues.

The BRF Prayer

Almighty God,
you have taught us that your word is a lamp for our
feet and a light for our path. Help us, and all who
prayerfully read your word, to deepen our
fellowship with you and with each other through your love.
And in so doing may we come to know you more fully,
love you more truly, and follow more faithfully in
the steps of your son Jesus Christ, who lives and
reigns with you and the Holy Spirit,
one God for evermore. Amen

A Prayer for Remembrance

Heavenly Father, we commit ourselves to work in
penitence and faith for reconciliation between the
nations, that all people may, together, live in
freedom, justice and peace. We pray for all who
in bereavement, disability and pain continue to
suffer the consequences of fighting and terror.
We remember with thanksgiving and sorrow those
whose lives, in world wars and conflicts past and
present, have been given and taken away.

From An Order of Service for Remembrance Sunday,
Churches Together in Britain and Ireland 2005

Retreat to focus on God

Society has become ever faster and more demanding of us all. We are pulled in different directions at the same time. If we are not careful, we can lose ourselves and our relationship with God without even noticing it because of the demands placed upon us by others and sometimes even by ourselves. No one is immune to these pressures. Whoever we are and whatever we do, we can be caught up in the stresses and strains of the world. In the midst of this busyness we can lose focus on the foundations of our faith.

Over the next fortnight we will have the opportunity to step aside from the stresses and strains we are under, if only for a short while, to deepen and possibly even rediscover that which provides our meaning and purpose in life: our relationship with God.

Deepening our relationship with God by going on 'retreat' has been part of the Christian tradition down the ages. This is not surprising, as we are copying Jesus. In three of the Gospels, Jesus himself prayed and fasted for 40 days in the wilderness (Matthew 4:1–11; Mark 1:12–13; Luke 4:1–13) in order to prepare himself for his public ministry. There are many other examples in the Gospels where Jesus and his disciples would take themselves physically away from the crowds to pray, often to refocus on the work that God was asking of them.

Jesus himself would go on overnight retreats: for instance, he went by himself 'out to the mountain to pray; and he spent the night in prayer to God' (Luke 6:12). On occasions, especially when things had been busy, he took his disciples with him: 'He said to them, "Come away to a deserted place all by yourselves and rest a while." For many were coming and going, and they had no leisure even to eat. And they went away in the boat to a deserted place by themselves' (Mark 6:31–32).

By going on retreat, many have drawn closer to God. In entering deeper into the mystery that is God they have started to find some of the answers to their lives. It is in that experience that these reflections are offered.

Unless otherwise stated, quotations are from the New Revised Standard Version of the Bible.

1 The wilderness experience

Matthew 4:1–11

In this passage Jesus speaks three times (vv. 4, 7, 10) and, in each case, answers the temptations placed before him by the devil with 'It is written…'. He thus answers the suggestions of the devil by reference to the scriptures that he has come to fulfil. In each instance Jesus refers to Deuteronomy and the testing of Israel in the wilderness after the crossing of the Red Sea, so, in reading this passage, we should be aware of Deuteronomy 8:2, which reminds us of that testing over a period of 40 years. Jesus takes on the role of Israel 'to be tempted' but, where Israel failed, Jesus is triumphant.

Matthew picks up the same sequence of events as Mark (1:12–13) but furnishes extra description. Luke (4:1–13) also uses the same material. However, Matthew places the wilderness experience between Jesus' baptism and the Sermon on the Mount, thus linking it with the crossing of the Red Sea and the giving of the law on Sinai.

We are caught in the same place. The 'wilderness experience' seems to loom large in many people's lives. For many, the inner wilderness is an experience of isolation in which we feel we are alone. This sense of isolation seems to be shared by most people, if not all, and therefore Jesus shares it with us. Furthermore, what happened to Jesus in the wilderness can give us insight into our own wilderness experience.

The same Spirit that had earlier come upon him at his baptism, calling him into his earthly ministry, now takes him into the wilderness (v. 1). So it is the same Spirit, given to us at our baptism, that leads us into our wilderness. It is in this wilderness that we will both find God and discover our calling. In feeling isolated or alone, we will come to depend upon God in a new and deeper way through that isolation and aloneness. Thus we will move from slavery into the promised land and the knowledge of the love of God.

What is your experience of inner wilderness, and have you met God through it?

2 Caught up in the world?

Matthew 6:25–34

We are challenged here in no uncertain terms not to be caught up in the concerns of the world. We should be exclusive in our desire to serve God: 'but strive first for the kingdom of God' (v. 33). The passage seems to hark back to a time in the early church when it was used as a teaching passage showing how God should always be uppermost before three basic worries of life: food, drink, clothing (v. 31).

The passage suggests that if only we could be single-minded in our devotion to God, we could put to one side our material worries. We are offered freedom from worry, not idleness, by the illustration of the birds, and are warned that we can add nothing to the length of our lives, however much we might try or want to (v. 27). But we are accused of being people of little faith (v. 30). It is in faith in God, and in seeking his kingdom, that we will no longer find ourselves worrying (vv. 33–34). This, though, is perhaps easier said than done, especially if we do not understand what worry is.

It is important to understand the difference, therefore, between being diligent and worrying. We are indeed called to take care and be diligent in all that we do, as God wants us to do things well in accordance with his will. Proverbs 21:5 tells us, 'The plans of the diligent lead surely to abundance, but everyone who is hasty comes only to want.' But we need to be careful that our care and diligence do not descend into anxiety and worry. It is seldom that something is done well which is done in haste and impetuosity, without wisdom (Proverbs 4:11–12). Instead of being caught up in the world and its demands, trying to answer instantaneously and driven by anxiety to respond without thinking, we should take our time to do things to the best of our abilities. Try, then, to take your time to make each decision quietly and in prayer, one at a time. In doing so, rely upon God's care, looking to him primarily in all that you do and all that you are.

How are you caught up in the concerns of the world? How far is God central to your life? Do you act in haste rather than carefully and diligently?

3 Travelling with God

Matthew 7:13–20

This passage poses us with a choice between two paths, one leading to destruction and the other to life. To make matters more difficult, we are told that there are those who are willing to mislead us in the choices that we have to make. We are called to make our judgment about those people by their actions rather than just their words.

This idea of 'two ways' is also found in the Old Testament (Deuteronomy 30:15; Jeremiah 21:8). In this passage from Matthew, life is to be found not by following the crowd but by a deliberate and costly decision to go the other way. True discipleship will be a minority decision, but the narrow gate is there for all to enter if and when they choose to divert from the wide and easy road.

The Old Testament also contains the idea of two types of teacher or prophet (Deuteronomy 13:1–5; 18:20–22). Here in Matthew, believers are being warned against following false teachers and prophets, who, in the past, have led others to destruction. The apostle John encourages the church to recognise true teachers as those who reveal God's love and live in the light (1 John 2:10). False teachers or prophets are to be recognised by their offering of an easier alternative to the narrow way of Christian discipleship.

We are thus called to follow the narrow way, manoeuvring between alternatives that will lead us away from discipleship. It is in a careful balancing act between deficiency and excess that we will find the way. As Gregory of Nyssa states in *The Life of Moses*, neither the wisdom of the serpent nor the innocence of the dove is to be praised if a person opts for one to the neglect of the other. We need to try and bring these two attitudes together; in doing so, we will find the virtue of the narrow gate. If we lack moderation, we will either become self-indulgent or live to excess: it is in the virtue of moderation that we discern God's calling.

In what areas of your life are you tempted to follow the crowd rather than taking the 'narrow' way? How can you live a balanced life of moderation rather than deficiency or excess?

4 Carrying heavy burdens

Matthew 11:28–30

There is no parallel to these verses in any of the other Gospels: they stand alone here in Matthew. Due to the content of the passage, it has been suggested that they are a later addition to the text. Their content is quite clear: Jesus is presented as the model on which to base our lives. The phrase that draws us to that realisation, 'for I am gentle and humble in heart' (v. 29), is so simple, yet many of us find it so difficult to put into practice.

Even though we 'know' God, we struggle to follow him in our lives (see Romans 7:15). Our difficulty may be increased by the way that we try to discern what God is asking of us. It is easy to fall into the trap of hearing what we want to hear. In doing so, we fail to 'learn from [him]' and act upon what we are being shown. We should realise, of course, that we are in good company, as the apostle Paul himself struggled in this way (Romans 7:18–25).

Despite the fact that God calls out to us, we are torn between the 'memory' of God in our lives—God's image in us—and the less godly things that we so often want to do. We can only cope with this situation by laying down the heavy burdens that we carry and falling upon God's mercy and grace. In doing so, we will find rest for our souls (v. 29). The yoke that Jesus is offering is not a complicated one; it is, rather, just the opposite. As we can see in Romans 13:9, it can be 'summed up' in one sentence: 'Love your neighbour as yourself.' That is our challenge, because in it is the fulfilling of the law and all that Jesus calls us to.

How do you prevent yourself from hearing what you want to hear rather than discerning God's true call? How do you prevent yourself from doing those things you want to do rather than those things that God calls you to do?

5 Standing before God

Matthew 16:24–28

This passage is stark in its challenge to us. To become a disciple of Christ, we need to give up everything. We are faced with the realisation that we no longer even belong to ourselves: 'You are not your own' (1 Corinthians 6:19). The command 'Take up your cross and follow me' (v. 24) does not allow any compromise. The cost of discipleship to us is death: there is no possibility of being a disciple and at the same time saving one's life. If we want to save our life, we cannot enter the kingdom; but, if we are willing to lose our life, we will find it (v. 25). Through poverty in this age we will find wealth and richness in the next (5:3). In this realisation we enter into the paradox of faith and the mystery which is God.

When coming on retreat, people entering into silence are often faced with this paradox. By entering into an inner solitude through such an experience, they are not entering a mere vacuum but are entering into the presence of God in order to stand before him. In deep silence and in inner solitude, our eyes become fixed upon God: wherever we turn, we find God. If we enter into the silence of a retreat without moving into this inner solitude, the experience falls short of what a retreat can be, and does not move us further forward. However, if we do enter into this inner solitude, it is everything, as we come into the Lord's presence. Surely, being in the presence of God, standing before him, is everything that we as disciples could desire.

How do you answer the challenge to give up everything? How do you enter into inner solitude before God?

6 Finding meaning and purpose

Matthew 12:46–50

The statement that Jesus makes in this passage, that his disciples are 'my mother and my brothers' (v. 50), is one of intense power. The only relationship that Jesus is shown to recognise comes about through common obedience to God. You can imagine that his physical mother and brothers were not particularly impressed by the situation, but the statement is not about their feelings: Jesus is not trying to be cruel. What he is showing through his words is that discipleship creates an even stronger tie than that created by family.

This statement, made in front of the crowds while his physical mother and brothers stand outside, is dramatic. His mother and brothers here represent the people of Israel who do not commit themselves wholly to him—whether through unbelief or a lack of understanding—while the crowds gathered around him represent his disciples and those who believe. The disciples are thus shown as being privileged because they are ones who 'do the will of my Father in heaven' (v. 50). Doing the 'will of the Father' is what counts. It is not about intellectual assent but, rather, about practical obedience. In such a relationship we find our true meaning and purpose.

It is in worship that many people find a sense of gathering around Christ today. In prayer and in worship we become one with each other and with God. Jesus prayed, 'As you, Father, are in me and I am in you, may they also be in us' (John 17:21): so we are called to be one with him, with God and with each other. In that oneness we will find our true meaning and purpose, bound to each other through love. It is in that moment that we will arrive at the goal our souls have yearned for.

Whom do we consider to be our 'mother and brothers' and how does that affect our relationship with them? How far are we one with God and with our fellow disciples, and how far do we hang back from being one with them?

Guidelines

Dorotheus of Gaza, one of the Desert Mothers, noticed something very interesting about those who swam in the sea, and used this observation as an analogy for the spiritual journey. She noticed that those who swam into the waves did not get very far and were soon worn out, while those who learnt to dip down below a wave and come up after it had gone over them could carry on swimming for much longer and much further. Many of us (and ministers are very much included in this) get caught up in urgent demands and plough on, come what may, getting things done as either we ourselves or the pressure from others drives us forward. We do not take time to dip below the wave to preserve and renew our spiritual energy. We are caught up in the world and in the agenda of the world rather than learning to challenge it and present the values of the kingdom of God. In doing so, we endanger our own walk as disciples. This is why finding time to go on retreat—or even just taking time wherever we are, in which we reconnect with our inner solitude—is so important. It is vital for our spiritual health.

In this week's readings we have been on a journey from the wilderness to find meaning and purpose in our lives. We have had various staging posts en route, which we may have found challenging as well as encouraging. But in our journey we have had a constant companion: Christ. He has drawn alongside us. 'While they were talking and discussing, Jesus himself came near and went with them' (Luke 24:15). We may or may not have recognised him but he has been there with us. Let us pray that we might notice our hearts burning within us, open our eyes and recognise the love of God that surrounds us (vv. 30–32).

1 Setting the agenda

Luke 4:16–30

It must have been an occasion where you could have heard a pin drop. Jesus stood in front of those who knew him and whom he knew. They were expecting great things from one of their own. It was in this moment that he would set the agenda for his ministry. The words that he spoke were inspirational but they were not what the people gathered in that synagogue in Nazareth wanted to hear—just the opposite. Truth, they say, hurts, and these words carried a message that must have hurt.

But what was so wrong with the words that Jesus said? What made his listeners so full of rage? What made them drive him out of town in order to hurl him off a cliff?

The difficulty is surely in the mirror that Jesus holds up to those who are listening to him. In identifying himself with the prophets, he identifies his audience with those who persecuted the prophets. To make matters worse, Jesus goes even further by reminding them that the only leper healed by Elisha was not Jewish but was a foreigner—the commander of the enemy army. This is what created the commotion and anger among the crowd at Nazareth. Jesus pointed out that God's agenda was not their agenda: God's agenda of grace was available for everyone.

This message, which is also found in the passage from Isaiah that Jesus read, acts as an incendiary, especially as he stops short of referring to the 'vengeance of our God' (Isaiah 61:2). The message of grace, and not vengeance, that Jesus proclaims challenges our understanding of what we want for ourselves: it challenges our interests and our agendas, replacing them with God's exciting and all-encompassing gift of grace.

How far, if you are honest, do you identify with those who heard Jesus speak that day and did not want to act upon his words? How far are you willing to replace your agenda with God's agenda of grace?

2 Proclamation of the kingdom of God

Luke 10:1–12

Jesus, in sending out the Seventy ahead of him, shows himself to be a master of the campaign trail. This number of assistants is significant as it is the same number that Moses called to help him to lead the Israelites into the promised land (Numbers 11:16). Jesus is thus sending them out to proclaim a new exodus. They are to urgently proclaim that 'the kingdom of God has come near to you' (vv. 9, 11).

Jesus was faced with the same difficulty that Moses encountered: those whom he wanted to lead in this new exodus just did not want to know, despite all that he had done for them. The teaching and the healings seemed to be for nothing. The people wanted something different: they wanted a political kingdom of God, not a heavenly or spiritual kingdom which had at its heart God's grace and love.

Therefore, the Seventy went out to both encourage and warn the villages and towns that they visited. They went with an urgent, stark choice. This would be the last-chance saloon for those to whom they ministered. Jesus was on his way to Jerusalem, and to reject him and the message he proclaimed was to reject God himself.

At the heart of this urgency is love proclaimed in hope. It is to that hope, despite the chaos and the struggle that so often surrounds it, that we should cling. Without that hope, which we can share with others, we will not realise the kingdom of God in the here and the now. If we can cling on to that hope, we will see the light of the dawn of the kingdom of

God in our lives before the Son of God comes again in his glory.

What is the kingdom of God for you? How far do we want the kingdom of God to dawn in our lives?

3 Building on firm foundations

Luke 6:46–49

The picture that Jesus creates for us in this passage is a vivid one. We can all picture the two houses—one built on firm foundations, surviving the torrent of water while the house without foundations is washed away. In this vivid picture Jesus is warning us against something that he is deadly serious about—the false teaching of others in opposition to his true teaching. And because the picture is so real, the warning is just as relevant to us today as it was to those who first heard it.

This parable presents us with a choice: we either conform our lives to the teaching of Christ or we do not. We cannot pick and choose. We cannot say that we will adopt this bit of Christ's teaching because it suits us while rejecting that bit because it does not. As William Temple wrote in *Mens Creatrix*, 'A sane man does not say, "The law of gravitation does not suit me, so I can ignore it and walk over the edge of this cliff in security"; nor will a sane man say, "A God who requires me to love my very tiresome neighbour and even my most wicked enemy does not suit me, so I will pursue my selfish interests in security."' Our actions ultimately do not make any difference to the reality of God and the purpose he is calling us into—to live in love (1 John 4:7–12).

Love conquers all, and it is on the foundations of love that we should build our lives. The love of God wants and desires us to flourish, reaching the full potential of what we are called to be. This is not a selfish love, which wants to manipulate us, but rather a love that grants us free will. It is revealed to us in the life of Christ and is made known by his life and death. In this love we are called into union with God and with our neighbour.

How far do you pursue your own attachments and selfish interests rather than the love of God? How far do you show God's love by loving your neighbours—even the ones you dislike—as you love yourself?

4 Caught up in the love of God

Luke 2:1–20

The relationship between Mary and Jesus was one of love. His conception had been supernatural, perplexing and probably very frightening for her. It had called for her to have a deep faith and to be obedient to God in a way that no other person has been called. Yet when Mary 'wrapped him in bands of cloth, and laid him in a manger' she did it out of love—as any mother or father would do for their child. She did not love her son, Jesus, because she felt that she ought to love him. She loved him because he was dear to her: he was her son.

We are told that she 'pondered' all the things that the shepherds told her 'in her heart' (v. 19). Later, when the twelve-year-old Jesus was found among the teachers in the temple, she 'treasured all these things in her heart' (2:51). Thus we can see in Mary not just a willingness to accept what is happening to her but a desire to reflect and dwell upon it. This is a model of faith for us to follow. As John Henry Newman points out in Sermon Number 15, for Mary it is not enough to possess faith; she uses it. It is not enough to assent to faith; she develops it. It is by standing at the foot of the cross and witnessing to Christ's resurrection that Mary will come to a fuller understanding and realise her love more fully. It is in this place, the place where we enter into deep worship, that we too will come to a greater realisation of our own faith.

We will then gradually move through the four stages of love in faith that Bernard of Clairvaux identifies. We will move from our selfish love of ourselves to a love of God for what he has done for us, then to a love of God for our relationship with him, and finally to the place where we can love ourselves simply due to the realisation that God loves us. In this fourth stage, we come to love ourselves with the same intensity of love that he gives us, entering into and sharing God's love. The mutuality of love transforms us and our relationship with God and with others as we participate in the action of God's love. We come to love those around us simply because God loves them.

How do you spend time 'pondering' on the work of God in your life and the lives of those around you? Do you love yourself simply because God does, or do you love yourself for your own sake?

5 Prayer

4 Caught up in the love of God

Luke 11:1–13

In prayer we should be—to use a very unfashionable word—disciplined, and we should persevere. The Lord's Prayer also demands that we face up to the reality of our lives, being honest with God about who we are.

Jesus is challenging us in saying that we should pray for forgiveness that reflects the way we forgive others. He demands that we should be more aware of who we are. By asking forgiveness for our sins each day, we are prevented from fantasising about our supposed innocence. Ultimately we cannot pretend that the skeletons in our closets are not there (we cannot hide them from God or from ourselves: 1 John 1:8–10), but we also need to realise that God is willing to forgive if we ask for his forgiveness. That forgiveness—or God's pardon—is assured by the promises that Jesus has given.

Jesus sets out the conditions under which we will be granted forgiveness. It is stated as a law but expressed as a covenant. We can only expect our sins to be forgiven according to the degree that we ourselves forgive sins that have been committed against us. We are told in no uncertain terms that we will not be able to gain what we ask—forgiveness of sins—unless we have forgiven those who have sinned against us (see also Matthew 7:2; 18:21–35; Mark 11:25). There is no room for excuses.

Jesus now calls us into a new relationship with others around us, bringing peace and renewing relationships. We who share in the one Spirit should be of one mind and one heart, united one with another and with him. He tells those who are not of one mind to leave their quarrels at the altar and first reconcile themselves to each other before they come to worship (Matthew 5:23–24). Prayer should thus be offered in a spirit of peace, having forgiven those who have sinned against us and having renewed our relationships.

How do you forgive others? Have you reconciled yourself to those who have sinned against you?

6 The giving of the Holy Spirit

Luke 24:44–49

Jesus states that he will send upon his followers what his Father has promised—the Holy Spirit—that they might be 'clothed with power from on high' (v. 49). The working out of that gift in the world is to be found in the Acts of the Apostles. The Holy Spirit closes the last gap and enables us to enter into a deeper relationship with God.

We are called by the power of the Holy Spirit to allow others to recognise the markers on the road, just as Christ did on the road to Emmaus (Luke 24:27) or when appearing in the upper room (vv. 44–45). We are called to work in harmony with God so that others may enter into a greater union with God. This, however, does not mean that all of our relationships will be cosy and without challenges. Just as Christ challenged those around him, so we will challenge those we meet, through the mediation of the Holy Spirit.

We are all called into a new relationship with God (John 15:15–17). We are to be his 'friends'. It is important to recognise that Jesus, through his ministry, met and befriended a wide range of people from soldiers to prostitutes, from Pharisees to Samaritans, and so we are called to do the same. He did not 'lord' it over them but met them as individuals, calling them into a new relationship with the holy. The Holy Spirit calls us into similar relationships with the people around us—even if we are only going to be a pale reflection of Jesus. At the heart of our relationships, as Aelred of Rievaulx reminds us in his work *On Spiritual Friendship*, should be loyalty, right intention, discretion and patience. Alongside these attributes should be a desire to be free of all those things that hold us back from the mutuality of love that we are called into by God. Ultimately, we are to model ourselves on Christ, forgiving and loving the people around us.

Do you befriend all or do you avoid some? Do you see Christ in all people, welcoming them as he welcomes you?

Guidelines

Over the last week we have explored a number of spiritual issues that seem to recur in people's lives. We have moved from setting the agenda ourselves to allowing God to do so, while recognising that we are called to model our lives on the life of Christ, so that we can live in the power of the Holy Spirit. Key to this is to understand how important relationships were for Jesus and, therefore, how important they should be for us. If only we can come to rely more fully upon God, we will then come to love more, and our anxieties will be lessened and our relationships with those around us changed. As we become more Christ-like, we will access at an ever deeper level the grace of God that knows no bounds.

If this transformative process is to continue to happen, so that we may be conformed more completely to God's calling, we need to open ourselves up to his presence. As we are changed continuously by God's grace, we will move further and deeper into his presence and increasingly become people of deep compassion for those around us and their needs. Our love for God and for all people will become the dominant voice in our lives as we come to share more fully the union of Christ. Through the grace of God we will become increasingly open-hearted and ready to show solidarity with his people—especially those who are marginalised by society. This may challenge us, as we will learn to love those whom we might not have chosen to love before. Perhaps, in rising to this challenge, the way that we pray for the blessing of God may become much wider, so that all people are included, not just those who are like us and whom we would choose to have as our friends.

Mark 6—8

In the previous set of studies on Mark (3:7—6:6a), we saw how Mark develops the themes that he introduced in his prologue (1:1–15). The good news of victory that the Gospel announces concerns the defeat of Satan and his demonic hordes. Jesus wages this war through his ministry of exorcism and teaching. The kingdom announced by Jesus will involve the punishment of the wicked, which includes sorting out the wheat from the chaff among God's own people. Jesus' teaching on the kingdom may be difficult, but accepting and living it will ultimately result in reward, and there is a hint that the kingdom is a more humble affair than many are expecting. Mark recounts Jesus' exorcisms and nature miracles in ways that demonstrate to the reader Jesus' true nature as the Lord God. This understanding is not accessible to the characters within the Gospel, however, who continue to puzzle over who Jesus is. Some find the puzzle too demanding and reject him (6:1–6a).

17–23 September

1 Rejection and commissioning

Mark 6:6b–13

Mark juxtaposes the story of the rejection of Jesus' ministry with this story of the commissioning of the twelve disciples. The folk of Jesus' home town did not accept his ministry, so he was able to heal only a few people there (6:5). He now commands his disciples to respond directly to the kind of welcome they get: if a place does not receive them or listen to them, they should wipe the dust off their feet on the way out; and in a place where people do receive them, they should remain in the welcoming household while they are in that town. Within ministry, then, Jesus recommends to his disciples that they broadcast the word evenly, but invest time in tending to those who want to receive and grow.

The sign of wiping dust off the feet has caused no small contention. An older generation of scholars argued that Jews wiped the dust off their feet when they left Gentile territory, so this was a sign that, in the judgment, God would treat the Jews who rejected the disciples' ministry as if they were Gentiles. However, the evidence for this interpretation is slender. We merely have texts (for example, *Mishnah Oholat* 2:3) which state that Gentile dust is unclean. Therefore, righteous Jews might well wish to wipe it from their feet, but this is not stated explicitly. The current generation of scholars prefer the idea that it is a warning of coming judgment, modelled on the sign of Nehemiah (Nehemiah 5:13). However, Nehemiah shook his mantle, not his sandals. Neither parallel is exact but the inexact parallels, taken together, imply that the dust-wiping is a sign of judgment, suggesting that God will not treat them as his people who are deserving of rescue and reward.

The idea that the disciples ought to leave people to the judgment they have chosen by their rejection of the message of repentance can seem harsh to our ears today. However, it is simply the practical counterpart to the model of ministry that we find in the parable of the sower. Mark clearly approves of the model. He closes this second commissioning account with a statement that the disciples went out and exercised effective ministries of preaching repentance and healing.

2 Who is Jesus?

Mark 6:14–29

The success of the disciples' mission seems to draw greater attention to Jesus and the discussion of who he is. The question of Jesus' identity is central to the Gospel of Mark: the first few words identify him as the Messiah, the Son of God (1:1). The reader knows this, but the characters involved in the story do not. The Gospel tells how those who encountered him either began to recognise him or failed to recognise him for who he really was. Mark now brings the question to the fore once again. Encountering this question through stories can help us, as readers, to note ways in which we, like some characters in the Gospel, may fail to recognise who he is, and what that means in practice.

The discussion of Jesus' identity leads Mark to note the reaction of Herod, who identifies Jesus as John the Baptist, whom he has beheaded

(v. 16). The story of the beheading of John is grisly. It recounts an action of pure injustice, inspired by malice and carried out through foolishness. The story has no happy ending and, despite the best efforts of some commentators, does not seem to be resolved elsewhere in the Gospel. We often expect Bible stories to find resolution through healing, forgiveness or reconciliation, but this story has no such conclusion. It ends with cruelty and the best efforts of the oppressed to put a dignified face on things. It acts as a stark reminder that such things do happen.

Mark places the story of John's death within the story of the disciples' mission, which opens in verses 7–13 and ends in verse 30. The effect of bracketing one story with the other signals to the reader that ministry and mission do not always have a happy ending on earth. Jesus and his disciples are enjoying public success and popularity for the moment, but the time will come when the tide turns. Herod's identification of Jesus as John, 'the one I beheaded', carries something of a threat. Herod may not carry out the threat—Mark will show Pilate as the executioner—but Mark uses it to foreshadow Jesus' death. Ministry and mission may have many high points but it would be rash to fail to acknowledge the cost.

3 Compassion and teaching

Mark 6:30–34

Mark now ends the story of the mission of the disciples (v. 30). They gather together and report back on their mission. Jesus' response suggests that they are tired and need recuperation after this busy time of ministry. He cares for their needs as ministers and missioners. He recognises how many people they have been ministering to, and acknowledges that they cannot take time out to look after their basic needs (just as in Mark 3:20, the response of people to the mission means that they are not getting enough time to eat). The detail that Jesus cares for his co-workers in the gospel and their basic physical needs is worth noting, particularly for any of us in ministry who have found it difficult to accept that Jesus wants to care for our needs.

This makes the grace of Jesus in the following verses all the more remarkable. The crowds second-guess where Jesus is taking his disciples and get there first, to greet them. Far from rebuking the crowds (a response of which Jesus proves himself perfectly capable elsewhere), he responds with compassion. The comment that the crowds are like sheep without a shepherd (v. 34) recalls Moses' concern that someone should succeed him as teacher and judge over God's people (Numbers 27:12–23). The language of Mark 6:34, *hos probata me echonta poimena* ('like sheep without a shepherd'), is closer to Numbers 27:17 than to any other Old Testament reference to shepherds. So Mark casts Jesus in the role of Joshua, the man whom God called to teach his commands to his people after Moses.

This creates interesting material for reflection. Today, there seems to be a general assumption that compassion leads to action, and ministries of action-based compassion are often contrasted with teaching ministries. Mark can teach us something here. Jesus has compassion on the crowds because they have no one to teach them God's commands and, thus, how to live life to the full. Perhaps, as churches, we need to recover the compassion necessary to teach.

4 God's provision

Mark 6:35–44

The story of the feeding of the 5000 receives more than its fair share of interpretations aimed at uncovering its deeper meaning or symbolism. I remember, as a secondary school teacher, laughing out loud at the comment of one Year 8 pupil:

Symbolic [interpretation] is a bit far-fetched as well because:
* *12 baskets*
* *12 tribes of Israel*
* *12 in a dozen*
* *12 is my age*
* *So what?*

There may be many allusions to many biblical stories in this wonderful text, but we need to be careful about interpreting its meaning in the light of any other text unless the parallel is so close that it calls out for such an interpretation. Of the various parallels suggested, the closest is the story of Elisha and the man from Baal-shalishah (2 Kings 4:42–44). In both stories, someone provides food for the hungry, including loaves (Mark 6:38; 2 Kings 4:42); Jesus commands his disciples to feed them, and Elisha commands his servant likewise (Mark 6:37; 2 Kings 4:42;); the disciples and servant express disbelief at the command (Mark 6:37; 2 Kings 4:43); the people are satisfied and there is food left over (Mark 6:42–43; 2 Kings 4:44). The story is one of a number in which Mark compares Jesus to Elisha—probably to indicate that, just as Elisha followed Elijah, so Jesus follows John the Baptist as the 'stronger one' about whom John prophesied (Mark 1:7–8).

Perhaps Mark placed this story immediately after the flashback to John's death to underline that the hideous and unresolved injustice meted out to John must not discourage the first readers of his Gospel (who may themselves have been suffering persecution, according to some scholars). John may have been murdered but he prophesied that a stronger one would come, and this one has come in the person of Jesus. God will achieve his purpose, and justice will be done.

Nonetheless, the story of the feeding of the 5000 and their families remains, above all else, a story of God's provision. God makes possible what seems impossible to humankind. Encouragingly, God does this with the resources that are actually available, even though they are basic and seem inadequate. The simplicity of the story could almost be offensive to many of us who are engaged in complex ministries with complicated resource needs, but it stands as a call to remember the nature and working of the God we worship.

5 Defeat of chaos

Mark 6:45–52

Mark uses an extraordinary word to describe the disciples' struggle to row their way through the storm: *basanidzo* ('torture'). The best explanation is that Mark is reading the event through the lens of God's battle with the mythical forces of chaos and evil, the sea and the dragon. In such stories (common in Ancient Near Eastern literature), God defeats the sea or a dragon or dragons, representing poetically his defeat of evil and death. For an Old Testament example, see Psalm 74:13–14, where God defeats the dragon Leviathan. The tempestuous sea takes on the mantle of the mythical chaos-sea, and Mark pictures it as a demonic horde.

When Jesus sees his disciples struggling on the sea (being tortured by the forces of evil), he comes to them. In recounting the miracle of walking on water, Mark chooses very specific words: *peripaton epi tes thalasses* ('walking on the sea'). These words are taken from Job 9:8 (LXX), in which God walks on the chaos-sea to defeat it. So Mark reads Jesus as God battling and defeating the forces of chaos to rescue his disciples. This reading of the event explains the odd detail of Jesus' intending to 'pass by' (v. 48). God passed by Moses when he revealed his glory and person to him (Exodus 34:5–6). Jesus' desire is to reveal his true nature to his disciples by walking on the water and saving them from destruction. In calling out '*ego eimi*' ('I AM' or possibly 'It's only me'), he assures them not only that he is not a malevolent spirit but also that he is their one true, saving God (recalling Exodus 3:14).

The disciples do not grasp the significance, however. Their minds are blown by the experience but they do not get it because they do not understand what happened with the bread (v. 52). Mark probably intends us to draw a parallel between God feeding his people with manna in the wilderness (Exodus 16) and the feeding of the 5000. Jesus keeps revealing himself as the saving God and yet his disciples do not recognise him. It is easy to criticise them in retrospect but not quite so easy to do better than them in practice. Jesus does not ask his disciples to believe simply in formal doctrine that he saves them from evil, but in lived experience. Identifying ourselves with the disciples may help us to ask questions about how far our own faith extends.

6 Teaching and healing

Mark 6:53–56

Jesus has tried twice to give his disciples rest. First they went to a deserted place in a boat, but the crowds caught up with them (6:32–33). Then

Jesus packed the disciples into a boat to get away after the feeding of the 5000 (6:45), with the effect that the disciples passed a horrendous night of fear. Bewildered, they arrive in Gennesaret to face more crowds.

The crowds in these texts are pictured as running. Earlier they ran around the lake to where they guessed Jesus would be going (Mark 6:33). Now they run around the region to where they know Jesus has gone (v. 55). This picture of the crowds offers an insight into their eagerness to encounter Jesus and have their friends, families and themselves benefit from his amazing healing powers.

But Mark uses the narrative to offer a subtle commentary on Jesus and his ministry. The crowds long even to touch the fringe of his garment in the hope of receiving the healing power emanating from it—much as the woman with the haemorrhage touched his clothes (5:28). The fringes on their garments were to remind God's people of all the commands of God, encouraging them to follow those commands rather than their own evil desires (Numbers 15:37–41). Mark notes that the healing ministry of Jesus is just one part of his ministry: his fringes remind us of his own commitment to live out and teach the truth of the commandments of God. They also point forward to the next chapter, where Jesus will estab-lish himself as the true teacher of the Torah, over and above his rivals.

Without wishing to over-read this detail, it does seem to tie together two key parts of ministry, which Jesus kept together but we sometimes separate. Mark makes a point of tying together Jesus' ministry of heal-ing and exorcism with his teaching ministry. Jesus' first exorcism takes place as he teaches (1:21–28). He consistently commissions the disciples to preach *and* exorcise (3:13–15; 6:7–13). The whole gospel involves coming into the obedience of faith as much as the wholeness of Christ's healing power.

Guidelines

There is a tendency among commentators to berate the disciples for their fear and failure to appreciate who Jesus really was and what he had come to do. Epithets such as 'thick-headed' are used without blinking an eye. I wish to dissociate myself from this trend in scholarship. I am not sure that I would have done very much better, had I been one of the twelve he originally called and commissioned.

The disciples are commissioned and given authority. They are excited by their ministry, which is evidently powerful and effective. They also find that such ministry is exhausting and that breaks are not always easy to come by. They find themselves in life-threatening situations and are set seemingly impossible tasks. Mark makes us only too aware that they live under the threat of execution for following their vocation.

Yet Jesus calls them to more. He calls them to recognise that he is God. Mark can see it and paints the stories beautifully, with Old Testament allusions that bring out the disciples' lack of understanding. Such artistic storytelling is easier with hindsight. I suspect that, like these disciples, I would have been loath to pay attention to intimations of divinity from this holy man. After all, that would seem to be attributing blasphemy to him, which would be insulting. Yet Jesus calls us all to this understanding, and more. He calls us all to recognise that what we believe of God, he can actually do for us. This remains a challenge to us in practice: it is easy simply to recognise his divinity as a doctrinal formula, but Jesus calls each and every one of us to much more than this.

1 Torah and the 'hedge'

Mark 7:1–5

The first five verses of this chapter set up the controversy that the rest of the chapter recounts. In order to appreciate the heart of the argument, we need to do some historical homework. There has been much scholarly debate since the late 1970s over the nature and practices of the Pharisees, with many challenging the stereotype of the nit-picking legalist, found in much Christian teaching, as historically untrue and anti-Semitic.

The first comment to make, then, is that the picture Mark paints here is perfectly plausible historically. We know from the Mishnah, the apocryphal book of Judith and an ancient letter called the *Letter of Aristeas* that the kind of washing customs Mark describes were current in the Judaism of Jesus (*Mishnah Hagigah* 2:5; *Mishnah Yadayim* 3:2; Judith 12:5–7; *Letter of Aristeas* 305–6). The fact that these regulations appear in the Mishnah (the codification of the traditions of the rabbis—the successors of the Pharisees—in the second century AD) suggests that Mark is correctly reporting them as the tradition of the elders (v. 5).

However, the more important issue is about understanding the motivation of the Pharisees. They were determined to build a 'hedge' around the Torah. The hedge was a series of secondary rules developed to ensure that faithful Jews could not possibly break the commandments of God. These rules covered difficult moral situations where commands seemed to clash or where it was not obvious what constituted obedience to the commandments. In formulating the rules, the Pharisees were little different from Christians who spell out how we can do the right thing in situations where the Bible does not clearly legislate (for example, not smoking tobacco; not drinking alcohol; voting left wing—all of which I have heard preached and taught as the only option for serious Christians). As we read this chapter, we might like to think through all the regulations we add to the teaching of Jesus and, for the moment, read the story from the standpoint of the Pharisees.

2 Command and tradition

Mark 7:5–8

We do not know the force with which the scribes and Pharisees asked their question in verse 5. It could have been pointed, worried or simply enquiring—Mark does not tell us. However, the force of Jesus' initial response is clear enough. He accuses the scribes and Pharisees of acting a part. In Greek, a *hupocrites* was an actor who would play different roles in a play, adopting a new mask for each role played. So the force of Jesus' criticism is to say that the Pharisees are playing a part rather than being real.

Jesus expounds this accusation through his quotation of Isaiah 29:13. The Pharisees are presenting themselves as the obedient servant of God ('honours me with the lips', v. 6; 'worships me', v. 7), but the reality is that they are only acting. Jesus' claim that their hearts are far from God does not concern their emotions alone, as the 'heart' means, primarily, the seat of the will. Jesus is claiming that they simply do not want to do what God wants. He expands this critique in the final line of the citation from Isaiah, which suggests that they teach human commandments as if they were God's commandments. Jesus then develops the criticism even further, claiming that they actually leave God's commandments behind in order to grasp hold of the traditions of human beings.

Stand with the Pharisees for just one moment. They are concerned that God's people should live in a just and righteous way, in order to please and honour God. To enable this lifestyle, they clarify murky points of the application of God's commands, so that his people may know in practice how to live out the life to which God calls them. The Pharisees apply themselves to this task with great energy and enthusiasm. Jesus' critique must have been felt as a stinging rebuke. He is saying that, in everything they do, they are turning their own ideal on its head: for all their commitment, they have ended up simply following each other and, in the process, ignoring God.

Before accusing the Pharisees of legalism, we might wish to address the beliefs and practices we commend. We might ask how far we are recommending people to attend to the commands of God and how far we are asking them to swallow the interpretations and applications that we have added to those commands.

3 Qorban

Mark 7:9–13
Jesus now substantiates his argument. He restates the accusation strongly: 'You cast aside the command of God so that you establish your tradition.' Note the use of 'your tradition' instead of 'human tradition' in verse 9. Jesus thus sharpens the accusation before giving his example.

First of all, Jesus mentions the commands of God that are being put aside: 'honour your parents' (Exodus 20:12; Deuteronomy 5:16) and 'whoever curses their parents shall be put to death' (Exodus 21:17; Leviticus 20:9). He has chosen one of the Ten Commandments and an equivalent command, the breach of which require the death penalty. He does not intend to quibble over more minor aspects of the Torah.

Then Jesus identifies the tradition of qorban as contravening these commandments. Second-temple Judaism allowed for the making of prohibitive vows, in which something was dedicated to the temple or to God and was therefore unavailable to be used by anyone else, unless the vow was dissolved by the priest (Philo, *Hypothetica* 7:5). Such vows took the form 'qorban [the thing being dedicated]'. The Pharisees evidently believed that such vows ought to be kept, and allowed them to stand even if the person making the vow thereby failed to meet their obligations to their own father and mother as enshrined in Torah. Jesus accuses them of supporting many such practices, through which people may evade their God-given responsibilities (those laid down in Torah) by following human traditions.

Honesty and the keeping of vows are virtues, and Jesus would have been unlikely to recommend dishonesty or wanton disregard for promises made to God. However, discussions about how to ensure faithful following of God had ended up condoning disobedience, so Jesus challenges the scribes and Pharisees to reconsider their values. Where might we need to hear the same challenge?

I wonder whether we have done something similar in our evaluation of Jesus' commands. Perhaps we have been so keen to emphasise his love in contrast to the 'legalism' of the Pharisees that we hardly notice, any more, that Jesus is defending obedience to the commandments of God. Our development of an ethic of love runs the risk of being a contemporary *qorban* if we do not acknowledge that love is inseparable from God's command. As Jesus affirms elsewhere, the whole Torah 'hangs on' love of God and love of neighbour (Matthew 22:40). Love does not supersede the commands of God but enables us to fulfil them.

4 Clean and unclean food

Mark 7:14–15

Jesus calls the crowd to himself and offers them a proverbial saying. There is a certain irony for today's reader in his initial call: 'Listen to me, all of you, and understand' (v. 14b). Understanding the proverb might be more difficult than it looks. The saying seems, on first reading, to be declaring all foods clean: what makes someone unclean is not what goes into their mouth. Such an interpretation seems to be highlighted in verse 19b. However, if this is right, then Jesus becomes remarkably hard to understand. If he is intending to declare all foods clean, then he is declaring Leviticus 11 to be wrong or simply not binding—able to be ignored. On any of these readings, Jesus is contradicting the commandments of God in favour of his own teaching. But ignoring the commandments of God in favour of their own teaching is precisely the criticism that Jesus has earlier levelled against the scribes and Pharisees (7:6–13). So, in delivering this proverbial saying, has Jesus now become the hypocrite?

Some scholars read the text this way and make critical comments about Jesus' self-contradiction, or suggest that Mark is responsible for the confusion, or claim that we are seeing the development of later Christian teaching here. None of these explanations gets around the difficulty that someone in the early Jesus movement, then, seems to have fallen into the same trap as the scribes and Pharisees. However, if Jesus was declaring all foods clean, we can only wonder why the early Christians got into such debate over clean and unclean food (see, for example, Acts 10:9–16; Romans 14:6) when their Lord and Master had made such a clear state-ment on the issue.

The confusion disappears if we look at the context of the saying. Jesus' debate with the scribes and Pharisees is about whether or not to observe their traditions about washing before eating (7:2–5). Once we recognise this context, there is no need to assume that Jesus is referring to the whole kosher system in verse 15. Rather, he is contrasting food eaten with unwashed hands ('what goes into the mouth'—the issue under discussion) with the evil that people do (probably meaning, for example, disobeying God's commandments by not honouring parents). On this reading, there is no contradiction, and Jesus' saying still leaves room for the debates that the early Gentile Christians had about how much Torah they needed to obey. Jesus is no hypocrite and he does expect his follow-ers to obey God's commands.

5 'All' food

Mark 7:17–19

Jesus' disciples ask for clarification of the saying in verse 15, which Jesus offers with ribald irony. He asks the disciples to think through what happens to food that enters the mouth (when it has been eaten with unwashed hands). It enters the bowels (not the heart) and exits from there into the toilet. This describes the physical process reasonably well, but the observation that the food bypasses the heart does not function simply as a physical description. Jesus is using the physical fact that food bypasses the heart to emphasise his point that food eaten with unwashed hands will not render somebody impure.

There is no small debate about the meaning of the phrase 'cleansing all foods' (v. 19b). As we saw in yesterday's reading, interpreters run the risk of having Jesus contradict his own key message in this text if they suggest that he is proclaiming the kosher laws null and void. Moreover, if Jesus is declaring them redundant, it becomes difficult to explain why they were still an issue in the early churches (see Acts 10:9–16; Romans 14:6). However, the phrase 'all food' does seem to refer to *all* food. An insight that might be helpful is the way in which we use words like 'all' and 'everyone'. Often we use them to refer to the whole of a particular group, as in the sentence, 'Everybody who is anybody was there.' Mark does use the Greek word for 'all' (*pan*) in this way elsewhere in the Gospel. For example, he has 'all' the sick and demon-possessed brought to Jesus for healing (1:32), yet another demoniac (5:3–5) has not encountered Jesus before. In 1:32, 'all' probably means all (or even 'many of') the demoniacs in the area of Capernaum—whereas the man possessed by Legion (5:3–5) lived on the other side of the Sea of Galilee. If Mark uses 'all' in this way to mean the whole of a previously stated or commonly understood group, then the most likely interpretation of 'all' in our text is that it refers to all kosher foods, whether they have been eaten with washed or unwashed hands.

This reading leaves us with Jesus as a rabbi who taught his Jewish contemporaries to obey rather than break Torah. Jesus' disagreement with the Pharisees was not a matter of love versus legalism. Rather, it was a question of who had correctly interpreted the commands of the living God, and Mark clearly believes that Jesus had done so. Contemporary

Christians, then, need to listen to the teachings of Jesus and obey them—especially where they may be in the habit of thinking that Christian ethics involves nothing more than doing what seems on the surface to be the most loving thing.

6 Real defilement

Mark 7:20–23

This reading constitutes the second half of Jesus' commentary on his proverb in verse 15. The first half of his commentary (vv. 17–19) examines what goes into someone without making them unclean. The second half examines what comes out of them and makes them unclean. He sets eating with unwashed hands against a list of vices that genuinely do make people unclean, according to his teaching.

Jesus gives some structure to his list of what really defiles people. He lists two sets of six vices. In the first set, the vices are in the plural (in Greek): sexual immoralities, thefts, murders, adulteries, grasping-nesses and malices. In the second set, they are in the singular (in Greek): deceit, indecency, envy (the evil eye), bad-mouthing people (or blasphemy), arrogance and stupidity. The list ranges more widely than the Ten Commandments but is clearly rooted in them: theft, murder, adultery, covetousness and possibly blasphemy are included. (Some read blasphemy as 'speaking against other people', as the list is outlining sins against other people rather than sins directly and exclusively against God.) Jesus describes these vices as evil reasonings that come out of people's minds (v. 21a: Jesus uses the word 'heart' but, in ancient Hebrew thought, the heart was the seat of the will). This ought to challenge us to examine the way we think and to evaluate the motives and attitudes behind our thoughts.

Each of us will find different vices more personally challenging. However, two that may stand out as offering a challenge to our culture are *pleonexiai* and *huperephania*. The first (*pleonexiai*, which I have translated 'grasping-nesses') refers to the continual desire for more, the hunger for power and the urge to assert ourselves. The second (*huperephania*, meaning 'arrogance') refers to the attempt to appear more than we really are. It would probably be realistic to say that aspects of these dispositions are valued and praised within our culture, even within some churches. However, Jesus labels them as vices.

Guidelines

The Jesus we encounter in Mark 7 may seem somewhat different from the Jesus who has appeared in some Christian theology and teaching over the last few decades. The latter brings a fresh message of the liberating love of God, over and against the binding legalism taught by the scribes and Pharisees. He teaches us that love supersedes the law and that our Christian living must be informed by what we understand to be the most loving thing to do. This understanding of Jesus may well 'liberate' us not only from Old Testament law but also from some traditional Christian ethics, which we may find constricting and anything but life-giving.

However, this Jesus belongs to a theological school of the 1960s popularised in John Robinson's book *Honest to God* (SCM, 1963). The Jesus of Mark teaches obedience to the commands of God, but stands against the regulations that have been added to God's commands and conflict with them. He teaches stripping back such regulations in order to ensure that we obey the commands of God. (He does not actually criticise the Pharisees for adding to the commands of God where they help people to obey God. Indeed, elsewhere he commends their teachings: see Matthew 23:2–3.) In the vice list offered in verses 21–22, Jesus outlines very clearly some areas of practical ethics.

I would contend that in our focus on being saved by God, some of us may forget that Jesus is serious about calling us to live a new life. We are capable of such misunderstanding that we do not even recognise this new lifestyle as part of our salvation. The Jesus of Mark is our risen Lord and he calls us now, as he called his first disciples, to live holy and righteous lives. He calls us to listen to his voice and learn how to live out God's commands. For any of us who have downplayed this aspect of our life of faith, a good place to start listening again to the commands of God is in the Sermon on the Mount (Matthew 5—7), reading small sections (even verses or half-verses), meditating on how we actually live our lives in the light of his teachings, and letting our meditations inform our prayers.

1 The children's food

Mark 7:24–30

Mark pictures Jesus as trying, again, to escape (v. 24b). Ever since sending the disciples out on mission, he has been trying to help them to rest. He took them to a quiet place (6:31) but the crowds got there first (v. 33). He taught and fed the crowds and sent his disciples away (v. 45) but they had a dreadful night. He took some time to pray (v. 46) but was soon ministering again (v. 54). Then he found himself in conflict in his teaching ministry (7:1–23) while defending some of his disciples. Now, perhaps, he is retiring to the region of Tyre to get some rest, expecting no ministry in a Gentile area.

Ministry in Tyre would have been difficult as there was some animosity between the Jews and the Tyrians (Josephus, *Against Apion* 1:13§70). This was caused, at least in part, by the fact that much of the agricultural produce of Galilee ended up in Tyre and Sidon (see Acts 12:20). The fact that the Jews needed to protect their food supply against this trade (Josephus, *Antiquities* 14.§196,§209) suggests that the trade was unpopular.

This context offers some perspective on Jesus' saying in verse 27, which otherwise can seem abrupt. Jesus' vocation is to Israel and therefore his reluctance to minister among the Gentiles is understandable: he wishes to be obedient to his God-given call. The term 'dog' would ordinarily be understood as abusive. (The fact that the Greek uses the diminutive *kunarion*, 'little doggie', makes no difference to the nature of the address.) However, the economic context of the saying suggests an interesting subtext: 'You Tyrians literally take the food from the mouths of the ordinary Jews to whom God has sent me to minister. What right have you to take their spiritual food too?' The language of the saying remains harsh, but Jesus is being grittily challenging rather than rude and somewhat racist. The woman's reply may have some humility about it: she accepts the rebuff ('you dog'), perhaps aware of the way her city treats Jewish Galileans, yet continues to plead for her daughter. Jesus finds himself unable to be anything but gracious in response.

2 A healing miracle

Mark 7:31–36

This healing story often appears odd, if not a little vulgar. Jesus sticks his fingers into the deaf man's ears (and the Greek word *ebalen*, meaning 'cast' or 'threw', does not suggest that he did this gently). He spits—possibly spitting on his fingers and then placing his spittle on the man's tongue, although the phrasing does not rule out his spitting on the ground or into the man's mouth. Then he groans or, possibly, sighs or wails.

Jesus does not behave in what we might judge to be a very seemly manner. Few churches today would encourage such behaviour as part of the ministry of healing. However, within Hellenistic culture and on the fringes of Judaism, the application of spittle as a means of healing was well known. Similarly, Hellenistic magical practitioners, who tried to gain control over spiritual powers to their own ends, are known to have sighed and wailed to gain spiritual power (PGM XIII:942–946; H.D. Betz, *The Greek Magical Papyri*, University of Chicago Press, 1992). We have no surviving record of any spell from the ancient world that parallels Jesus' actions here, so we cannot claim that Jesus was using an ancient magical ritual. However, his actions certainly seem akin to what other healers of the time did, and in this story he seems to be working within the cultural idiom.

The healing ritual works. The man who could only speak a little or with difficulty (v. 32, *mogilalos*, 'speaking only a little, speaking with difficulty') can now speak properly (v. 35). This man who was deaf can now hear. The crowd react with understandable enthusiasm. Jesus repeatedly tells the crowd not to make the miracle known and the crowd repeatedly ignore his instructions. (The Greek tenses used by Mark give us the impression that the reaction of the crowd took place over a period of time.) However strange the story may appear to us, the crowd's behaviour is instructive. Where God is at work to save and to heal—however odd the medium may seem—rejoicing is the appropriate response.

3 Mark and Isaiah

The response of the crowd may have been triggered by an insight going beyond the miracle itself. This healing miracle recalls the text of Isaiah 35:5–6 (LXX). The picture that Isaiah paints of the age to come has the stammerers (*mogilaloi*) speaking clearly and the deaf (*kophoi*) hearing. It depicts what life will be like when God restores the political fortunes of Israel and gives his people peace and prosperity. The crowd witnessing Jesus' miracle appear to have noticed this connection and cannot restrain their excitement at the prospect that freedom and prosperity have come at last: God has acted on behalf of his people.

The way in which the story is told also signals that Mark intends us to make the link with Isaiah. There are enough parallels between this miracle and the healing of the blind man in 8:22–26 to suggest that Mark wants us to see him pairing these events. Both stories include the phrase 'and they brought him' (*kai pherousin auto*), as well as the phrase 'and they beseeched him that' (*kai parakalousin hina*); both use a compound of the Greek word for 'receive', *lambano* (*apolabomenos*, 'taking aside', in 7:33; *epilabomenos*, 'took by the hand', in 8:23); both include 'and having spat' (*kai ptusas*); both have 'and looking up' (*kai anablepsas*). So Mark links the healing of the deaf and stammering man with the healing of the blind man—and all three conditions are healed in Isaiah 35:5–6.

The crowd's acclamation overstates the case, however. Jesus did not heal someone who could not speak (*alalos*) but someone who spoke with difficulty (*mogilalos*), yet the crowd says that Jesus can make the dumb (*alalos*) speak. Although Jesus does fulfil the expectations and hopes of the crowd that he has come to bring in God's new age, he does not fulfil their expectations exactly. Perhaps Mark is preparing his audience here for the teaching that Jesus will soon deliver (starting at 8:22), that the way in which God has chosen to fulfil his promises will not fully coincide with what his people want and expect. This is a difficult lesson, which we would do well to continue to learn.

4 Feeding 4000

Mark 8:1–9

In his opening sentence, Mark tells us that we have been here before. The word 'again' next to the phrase 'there was a large crowd' suggests that we are to recall the feeding of the 5000 (6:35–44). Reading the stories together gives us a sharper insight into what might be going on in this second feeding story.

The disciples' question (v. 4) seems odd at first. Why worry about feeding 4000 people when they have already fed 5000? Have they learned nothing? Actually, they have learned. Last time, they suggested in disbelief that they would need half a year's wages to pay for the food (6:37b). This time, they ask Jesus where the food will come from: they seem to be aware that it can appear from somewhere, although they themselves clearly do not know where. This time, Jesus asks them how much food they themselves have (v. 5a), choosing to use their resources rather than asking them to pool whatever resources are available. Not only does he ask for their bread (vv. 5–6) but he also takes their fish (v. 7). They have ministered with the resources of others, and now he teaches them how he can minister miraculously from their own resources.

The miraculous nature of the ministry is highlighted in the final verses. Last time, twelve picnic baskets (*kophinos*) of leftovers were collected. This time, seven large baskets (*spuris*) are collected: some of these baskets were big enough to hold an adult human (as in Acts 9:25). The crowd have eaten their fill (v. 8), but the story does not end until Jesus has sent them away (v. 9b). This ending takes us back to where the story began. Jesus felt unable to send the crowd away because they had not eaten and some of them had long journeys ahead (vv. 2–3). He had compassion on them, and only when this compassion has been turned into practical action, which meets the human need, can the story truly be said to have ended.

5 Signs and prophets

The image of getting into the boat and crossing the Sea of Galilee brackets this story. First Jesus embarks and goes to Dalmanutha (v. 11) and then he embarks and goes to the other side (v. 13). This inclusion wraps itself around a brief controversy in which the Pharisees ask for a sign from Jesus and he berates them with his reply.

The background to this question may be found in the stories that the Jewish historian Josephus tells about Jewish sign-prophets. One such tells the story of Theudas, who persuaded many Jews to follow him to the Jordan, which he promised to part so that they could pass through. Theudas spoke of this sign to encourage his followers to revolt and fight in the 'second exodus'. The Roman procurator Fadus certainly understood the sign in this way, as he ordered a detachment of cavalry to kill and capture Theudas and his followers (Josephus, *Antiquities* 20:5.1§97–99). Another sign-prophet, referred to as 'the Egyptian', encouraged his followers to go with him to the Mount of Olives, from where he would cause the walls of Jerusalem to fall down so that they could take the city from the Romans. This time, the Roman governor Felix crushed the rebellion (Josephus, *Antiquities* 20:8:6§169–172). These sign-prophets performed signs reminiscent of the exodus and the entry into Canaan. Jesus, however, refuses to give such a sign—possibly because he is not leading a military revolt.

The irony, of course, is that Jesus has given an exodus type of sign twice already. He has fed the 5000 (6:35–44) and he has fed the 4000 (8:1–9). However, his motivations and hopes are far from rebellion. The Gospel of John records that, after the feeding of the 5000, Jesus withdrew from the crowd as they tried to make him king (John 6:15). We can misread Jesus' signs in order to attempt to bring his mission in line with ours, but the truth is that the gospel will march forward in the way that God wills.

6 Failure to understand

This puzzling little passage becomes all the more perplexing in translation because commentators and translators add the phrase 'it is because' to verse 16, which is not present in the Greek—presumably to make sense of the text. This verse reads literally, 'and they were discussing among themselves that they had no bread'. Translators, failing to see a commenction between this and Jesus' comment in verse 15, add words to make a connection. However, the disciples have made no such connection, and that is precisely the issue.

There are two different conversations going on here. Jesus is trying to instruct his disciples and reveal himself to them. The disciples are worried about their packed lunch: they have one bun (the 'bread' is more like a Spanish *pan* than an English loaf) between 13 people. Mark enjoys the irony, given that this discussion fairly closely follows the story of the feeding of the 4000. The disciples have seen two miracles in which thousands of people were fed, and they are still worried about how the 13 of them are going to eat their fill from one bread roll.

The most plausible current theory about the meaning of Jesus' comment in verse 15 is that the Pharisees saw themselves as the yeast that would leaven Israel—that is, make it holy through true obedience to Torah. Whatever the meaning, however, Jesus wants his disciples to understand who he is. The motifs of a failure to understand and a hardening of the heart (v. 17) have occurred together before, at 6:52. There, the disciples did not see that Jesus was walking on the water to reveal his divinity. Here, they do not make the connection because they do not see the significance of the feeding miracles, which is that Jesus has taken the role of God during the exodus, feeding his people in the wilderness.

In verses 19–20, Jesus asks his disciples questions to help them understand the significance of these miracles. They can answer the questions but they do not seem to grasp the truth to which they point—that Jesus is the Lord God of heaven and earth.

Guidelines

A storm is brewing. The ministry continues to be busy. Jesus and his disciples are in great demand—such demand that Mark depicts them as chasing rest, often without great success. The miracle-working ministry becomes more remarkable, and through it Jesus shows more of the generosity and grace of God.

Jesus shows more than this through the miracles, however. In this week's readings, Mark builds on the message he has begun to convey through the miracles. He tells the stories of the feeding of the 5000 and the walking on water to reveal that Jesus is God. He tells the story of the 4000 to reinforce the same message. He tells the story of the healing of the deaf stammerer in order to show that the eschatological age is dawning: Jesus will fulfil all the promises in the prophecies of Isaiah and others, about the day when God will save and restore his people.

Mark also lets us know that the crowd will not have their desires fully met. Jesus' mission differs in some respects from their hopes. The crowd overplay the miracle of the healing of the deaf stammerer: they see what they want to see. The Pharisees want an exodus miracle that points to the promised political freedom, whereas Jesus feeds his followers—those who are seeking to learn how to live the way God wants them to live. Despite the fact that the Pharisees do not recognise the signs of the feeding miracles, Jesus has given his own exodus signs. The disciples have their heads stuck in their picnic basket and so they fail to see what Jesus longs to reveal to them about himself and his ministry among them.

Mark leaves this first half of the Gospel by posing the question 'Do you not yet understand?' (8:21). The question introduces his audience to the key theme of what follows. The rest of the Gospel reveals the shocking news (shocking to first-century Jews, at least) of how God intends to save his people. This story takes us right to the heart of God.

FURTHER READING

Jacob Neusner, *The Mishnah: A New Translation*, Yale University Press, 1988.

The Song of Songs

The Song of Songs is a truly fascinating, if neglected, biblical book. It stands on its own, for it makes no connections to the history and religion of Israel (except for the 'Solomon' references). It does not mention God, the covenant or even Israel. It is love poetry. So why is it in the Bible?

One answer is that it claims to be Solomon's work, for the first verse reads, 'The song of songs [i.e. the best song] which is Solomon's', and elsewhere there are references to him (especially 3:6–11), and any words from King Solomon would have been greatly prized. It is also true that from earliest times, certainly among Jewish scholars around the time of Jesus, it has been interpreted allegorically as being about God and his people. Perhaps both of these answers, though, miss the very point of the Song—that the longing, passion and love between a man and a woman point us to God. There is a book about human passion, love and sex in the Bible because this is some of the richest language we have for speaking about God. Or perhaps it is simply because they are such important aspects of human life.

We have no clues to the book's authorship. The references to Solomon use him as an image of a glorious king, and one known for having many women (1 Kings 11:1–3), rather than asserting his authorship. Nor does the book give any hints to its date or setting. Its unity can also be questioned: there is certainly no overall narrative. Various ideas and phrases reappear throughout, there is logic within individual sections of the text, and the first and last chapters do seem to introduce and conclude the work. Nevertheless, it is hard to discern any real structure within. Many scholars therefore conclude that it is a collection of love poetry edited together, although there is no reason not to see it as the work of a single poet. Large parts of the text are written from the woman's perspective, which is very rare in the Bible (except for Ruth). It is perhaps rash to claim female authorship on these grounds, but it may well be the case.

Two methods of interpretation have dominated readings of the Song. For some, attempts to read it as anything other than love poetry do violence to it and seek wrongly to 'spiritualise' it. On the other hand, its place within the Bible has caused many interpreters, Jewish as well as Christian, to see it as speaking of God's relationship with humanity, since the husband–wife image is used to describe that relationship elsewhere (for example, Hosea 2—3; Ephesians 5:31–32; Revelation 21:2). The approach taken in these notes is to hold the two methods together. We will consider each part of the Song twice—first reading it literally as love poetry, then reconsidering it as speaking about us and God. Thus we allow the love poetry truly to breathe and be taken seriously, but we allow that very poetry to give us deeper meaning. Perhaps, at the end of these two weeks, you will have come to your own conclusion as to how best to read the Song of Songs.

Quotations are taken from the New Revised Standard Version of the Bible.

1 Yearning for love

Song of Songs 1:1—2:2

Immediately we are plunged into the heart of the Song, in structure and in content. The first word in Hebrew, after the title, is 'Let him kiss' or 'O that he would kiss': we are left in no doubt that love in all its physicality is the theme. That simplicity is not matched by the structure, though. As we read this first chapter, pronouns jump back and forward—we, you, I—and it is hard to pin down who is speaking. Careful reading seems to identify the woman in 1:2–7, 12–14, 16–17 and 2:1, 3; and the man in 1:8–11, 15 and 2:2, but who are the 'we' in the second half of verse 4?

We should be willing to let the Song be, on its own terms. It does not come to us as a drama with clearly demarcated voices, however natural that seems to us. There is a melding together of the man's and woman's voices; it is a song about their love, and about love itself, so why seek to divide what God has brought together (to steal a line from the wedding service)? This melding together highlights that their love is mutual: they long for each other; they describe each other in sensuous terms. This is an important point in our culture, which has tended to demarcate male and female roles: women dress up and men do the chasing, for example. We may think of ancient Israel as a patriarchal society, yet here we see love depicted more freely, pointing back to the mutuality of man and woman at creation (Genesis 1:27–28; 2:23–24).

The lovers' words convey a deep sense of yearning, of desire. 'O that he would kiss me,' the woman says (v. 1), and 'let us make haste' (v. 4); there are teasing arrangements for a meeting (vv. 7–8) and a sense of intimacy, even when presumably they are apart (v. 13). Desire sometimes gets a bad name, as if 'desire' always means 'a lust for something wicked'—as if 'our heart's desires' will be for a Mercedes Benz (in the words of the song), or for our own gratification or power. But the Hebrew Wisdom tradition speaks favourably of 'our heart's desire' (Psalm 20:4, Proverbs 11:23), and Christian traditions such as the Ignatian see the identification and befriending of our desire as crucial for our development as human friends of God. We see here how the woman's lack of confidence about her looks (vv. 5–6) can be overcome by the man's longing for her. Lovers' longing for each other is a good thing.

2 Yearning for God

Song of Songs 1:1—2:2

What do we make of these verses as a description of the relationship between God and humanity, or between a person and God?

Suddenly words like 'mutuality' become alive with theological meaning and challenge. It is striking to see the sense of mutuality—mutual desire and longing—depicted between a woman and a man; striking in an ancient text from a patriarchal world, and striking still today. But it is far more challenging to think of God yearning for us as we yearn for him.

Our ways of thinking about God have been dominated by philosophy. Theology is often defined as the 'rational study of God'. The Greek word on which it is based is composed of *theos* (God) and *logia*, which can just mean 'words' but generally means 'discourse' or 'rational discussion'. Before Jesus, and certainly in the usage of early Christian (Greek) thinkers, 'theology' meant 'reasoning about God' (or the gods). This approach has continued in our scientific age, in which 'God' has started to overlap with 'the laws of nature' and we have connected the idea of justice with objectivity and indifference (as in 'a lack of personal connection').

Many aspects of Christian theology challenge this idea. Jesus depicts God in personal terms, encouraging his followers to call him 'my Father' and telling the story of an emotional dad, rejoicing to have his wayward son return. The Song of Songs pushes this depiction further, for it speaks not just of our yearning for God, but of God desiring us for his own pleasure and satisfaction. He is lacking if we are not with him. The man in the Song is not a rugged, unmoved and distant object of the woman's desire, taken from some work of romantic fiction. The yearning and desire are not just one-way.

It's mindblowing to think that the Creator of the universe desires me with passion and longing. Yes, we desire him (how many modern worship songs say the equivalent of 'O that God would kiss me'?) and are hesitant about our worthiness (vv. 5–6), but let us listen and savour his desire for us.

3 The power of love

Song of Songs 2:3—3:5

This section of the text weaves around the repeated plea to the 'daughters of Jerusalem' not to 'stir up or awaken love until it is ready' (2:7; 3:5).

The woman's desire for her lover is so great that she describes herself as 'faint with love', or, as we might say, 'love-sick'. She asks for exotic food (2:5) but, as the following verses make clear, paradoxically the only cure for love-sickness is love. In the later part (3:1–5) she seems to be longing for him at night. The only cure is for her to search for him (vv. 2–3), find him and not let go (v. 4). In between we have the description of a meeting, culminating in 2:16–17, which it is probably right to interpret as sexual love-making—the man 'browsing [feeding] among the lilies' until day comes. Earlier (vv. 1–2), the woman herself was described as a lily.

The sequence within this section is intriguing. She is love-sick, then we hear the description of a meeting, and then she is yearning and searching for him. Perhaps the sexual encounter has already happened: it did 'stir up love', so now she is 'love-sick'—desperate for him, searching for him. Thus verses 8–17 would be a memory, which is causing her love-sickness. Once their physical love has been tasted, nothing else will satisfy. Or perhaps we should read verses 8–17 not as memory but as fantasy. It is this kind of meeting that she longs for. Both possibilities are true to experience. Yearning for physical, sexual love is only temporarily satisfied by its fulfilment. Desire for what you have not yet had, and desire for more of what you have had, can be similar.

The impact of this section is rather teasing—a warning not to awaken love, surrounding descriptions that make it seem very desirable! It's like the youth leader saying to the teenagers, 'Sex is great, but you are best leaving it until you are older/married.' Or perhaps we should read the plea not to awaken love as a kind of inverted boasting: 'My lover is so good, it's dangerous.' Teasing or not, there is truth here. Physical love, desire and sexual pleasure are powerful forces. There is no sense in the Song that they should be denied; but there is warning. We could also stress the words 'until it is ready': true love, desirable and powerful as it is, cannot be artificially created. We cannot find a sexual partner simply because we want one—or, at least, the Song warns us if we do.

4 Finding God

Song of Songs 2:3—3:5

How can we interpret these verses as speaking of the relationship between God and humanity? What is the spiritual equivalent of being love-sick (2:5), or of not finding God easily (3:1–4), or of the warning 'not to stir up love until it is ready' (2:7; 3:5)?

I can suggest three possibilities. First, we should remember those who seek God but feel that they don't find him. It is easy for us to say on theological principle that God is always found by those who seek him (Matthew 7:7–8; Revelation 3:20), but there are many who genuinely 'wish they could' believe. Perhaps in the words of the Song we can grasp something of this heartfelt, unconsummated desire for God—the good news being, of course, that in the Song the love does in the end find fulfilment. Love is not to be awoken 'until it is ready': those who desire God will find him; the time will come, but we cannot force it.

Second, we can follow the interpretation that 2:8–17 describes a real meeting between the man and woman: the longing is for pleasure and fulfilment once experienced but now denied. Here we can perhaps see into the situation of those whose faith has grown cold or who have been overwhelmed by events, such that they feel estranged from God. There remains a desire or yearning for something that is now beyond their grasp.

Third, the power of the emotion described in these verses can cause us to review our own relationship with God and recognise its limitations. If, like me, you read these verses and think, 'Yes, I can understand this about physical or sexual love, but not about love for God', perhaps you need to ask why. Why is our love for God often unemotional? Why does it not threaten to overwhelm us, make us faint, and cause us to search for him whenever we feel an absence? Rather than concluding that these words in the Song can't really apply to the relationship between us and God, perhaps we should ask why our relationship with God doesn't match up to the words in the Song. In the case of physical lovers, spending intimate time together is crucial to developing understanding and appreciation for each other, as we see in 2:8–17. Perhaps that is a message for us in our relationship with God.

5 Consummation

Song of Songs 3:6—5:1

The first part of this passage (3:6–11) describes the man's approach, using the imagery of King Solomon's procession. This section is clearly distinct from what has come before and what comes after, and some scholars see it as a pre-existing unit, which fits here slightly awkwardly. This is the only place in the Song where a wedding or marriage is mentioned, and even here it does not say that the man is approaching for his wedding, only that the Solomon figure is wearing a crown that he received on his wedding day. The Song is not a good place to find biblical verses to support the mantra 'No sex before marriage; after marriage it will all be great.' That is not to say it is arguing for anything different, merely that it is exploring love and desire openly and genuinely. While I would support traditional Christian teaching on sex and marriage, it is worth pondering that we are perhaps more obsessed by boundaries and rules than the Song is. Are we frightened to talk of love and desire?

The praise of the man here is really praise of his power, strength and wealth. In contrast, the praise of the woman that follows in the next distinct section (4:1—5:1) focuses on her physical beauty. We may feel that this is rather old-fashioned or stereotypical, but many of us would recognise that, for all our belief in equality between the sexes, men and women are attracted to each other by different qualities.

The praise of the woman is an elaborate set of comparisons drawn from the natural world. Generally we can see the point of each one, even if some are peculiar, like verse 4. Is it flattering for one's neck to be compared to David's tower, hung with shields? Presumably this refers to a graceful, straight neck adorned with necklaces. Some seem particularly sexual: for example, where the man says he will go 'to the mountain of myrrh and the hill of incense' all night (v. 6). The image of the enclosed garden and fountain (vv. 12–16) highlights that the woman belongs to the man alone (see Proverbs 5:15–19 for similar imagery), while also describing a fantasy of paradise.

Surprisingly briefly, we have the woman's invitation to the man to come as she offers herself (v. 16b), followed by confirmation that the man has indeed taken her (5:1). The final sentence should probably be seen as an aside by the author, affirming the lovers' mutual pleasure in each other. Although much of the imagery is alien to us, there is a boldness in this passage's affirmation of physical and sexual desire, mutual invitation and consummation. There is no shame.

6 God's passionate love

Song of Songs 3:6—5:1

If we are reading the Song as speaking figuratively of the relationship between human and God, the first part of this section (3:6–11) causes us no particular difficulties. It is praise of God through royal imagery (comparable, perhaps, to Psalm 24:7–10; Psalm 47). What is more challenging is the extent and nature of the man's admiration of the woman (4:1–16), for, on this reading, we should hear these verses as God's thoughts about us.

It is worth trying to read these verses in such a way. The rich extended description prevents us from saying, 'God loves me and thinks I am precious' and just moving on, the words slipping easily off our Teflon-coated wounded self-image as mere theological waffle. We all seem to have a sense of our own unloveliness, that we are deeply marred and barely worth loving—at least, if people saw us as we really are. This is why there is such joy in marriage, where we find someone who is willing to—indeed, wants to—make unlimited commitments to us, offering themselves to us, promising to love, comfort, honour and protect us. Yet these words in the Song would be addressed to us by the Creator of the world, from whom no secrets are hidden.

Of course, the description here is mainly a physical description of a young woman, which means that it makes complicated reading for men. As a man, it's hard for me to think that God says my breasts are like two fawns (though, I accept, it will be hard for most women, too!). We might also question the appropriateness of such a focus on physical attraction. But at some level this is to miss the point; indeed, our wounded self-image works hard to avoid accepting the message of God's passionate love for us, just as we are.

There is an energy in this poem, in which the full power of physical attraction and beauty is harnessed to express God's thoughts towards us—his love for us, his delight in us, his desire for us. All we need do, as the woman does in the poem, is to invite him in (4:16b) and he will come (5:1). Dare you believe that God considers you as beautiful and desirable as, in this section, the man does the woman?

Guidelines

Throughout the Song of Songs, so many of the images of love, and the lovers' physical descriptions of each other, are drawn from the natural world—wine and perfumes, birds and flowers. In part, we can say that this simply reflects the Song's origins in a more agricultural society, one that was 'closer to nature' that the urbanised life most of us now lead. That may be true, yet by reading the Song we are reminded of our unity with the rest of creation. Human love, which the Song extols as the ultimate in human life, pointing us to God, finds its voice through parallels with the rest of creation.

There is a great value in reflecting on this unity with creation; too much in our world today seems to separate us off from the rest of the created order, as we also contribute much to its destruction. The Song, though, takes this one step further by suggesting that it is good for desire, love and passion between a man and a woman to be 'natural' and even 'animal'. We are not on a quest to 'raise ourselves', by our intellect or supposed civilisation, from being as physical as the rest of God's good creation. The 'animal' element of physical love—the desire that we cannot control, the raw physicality of sex—has often caused great awkwardness, embarrassment and repression within the Church. Why? Why can we not celebrate and rejoice in this aspect of our creation? Maybe the attempt to hide our animal physicality is part of our fatal desire to make ourselves equal to God (Genesis 3:5–6), to escape from our created world by building a tower to heaven (Genesis 11:4).

What would it mean for you to be more accepting of your nature as a physical being, as part of creation? In what ways might you wrongly try to repress or ignore the 'natural' and 'animal' in your make up?

1 Love's trials

Song of Songs 5:2—6:3

Here we have another clear section of the Song; a dialogue between the woman and the 'daughters of Jerusalem', describing a failed meeting between the woman and her lover (5:2–6), followed by her search for him (vv. 6–16), culminating in an assertion that, absent or not, the lover is hers (6:2–3). There are parallels between this section and 3:1–5, which also begins with the woman on her bed and includes a search, but in 3:1–5 there is no 'refusal' and the search is successful. It does not make much sense to try to see this section as describing events that follow on from those earlier in the Song; it is better seen as an 'alternative future' or, at least, another commonly experienced facet of love.

In 5:2–5 we find the sequence of events that lead to the disaster. He asks for entry, she refuses, he tries to enter anyway, she decides to let him in, but he has gone. Ostensibly this is about entry into a house, though it is hard not to see a deliberate ambiguity here for sex, with the language of penetration and the woman opening herself. The hint is, presumably, that even if the description is about her opening the door, if she had done so it would soon have led to sex.

The woman's excuse for not opening (v. 3) seems rather pathetic, as indeed does his reason for wanting to come in (v. 2). Perhaps we should read both as something of a tease. Somehow, though, it goes wrong. Someone has misinterpreted something, and he is gone.

This sense of things just not working out—something that seemed so right somehow falling apart—is not uncommon in love and more generally in our lives. They both really wanted the same thing, but somehow misunderstanding crept in: she was waiting for him to phone her but he had lost her number and it just never happened; she kept on making a point of flirting with him but he thought she was just being friendly and was out of his league, and eventually things moved on. In other areas of life, too, we often experience situations that 'should have' worked out but just didn't, for no good reason.

Of course, the section finishes with the woman's assertion that, in the end, the man is her lover and she is his (6:2–3). Despite the unfortunate misunderstanding, they are really still together—an image, perhaps, of true love, which copes with the failures and mistakes. Even if, as a result of the description of his beauty, other women want to search for him as well (6:1), the woman is confident that they belong to each other.

2 Opportunity missed

Song of Songs 5:2—6:3

It is a sad truth of pastoral and evangelistic ministry that there are times when people are close to responding to God, stepping out in faith, opening the door to Jesus' knocking (5:2; compare Revelation 3:20), but the 'window of opportunity' does not stay open for ever. Often the final step is not taken, and then life happens and it is many years before the same opportune moment comes back. We may see it in the story of Zacchaeus (Luke 19:1–10). Jesus was passing through Jericho that day; the next day would be too late. If Zacchaeus wanted to see Jesus, he had to climb that tree now; now was the moment for the chance meeting to take place.

The woman in the Song did really want to 'open' for her man, but somehow, in the confusion, it didn't happen and then he was gone. That, too, can be the experience of many turning to God. They come to a point of recognising their need for God and their desire for him, yet somehow, when they get round to thinking about it more, the sense of God's presence has gone. Why? Surely, if God wanted them, he would still be there, wouldn't he? Surely he would be waiting for the moment, whenever it came, when they decided to turn to him. Theologically I might want to say yes, but pastorally I know that the answer is no. Sometimes, when people tell God to wait, they find that he isn't there when they finally turn round; the opportunity of connection has passed. They are still left with a positive sense of God, matching the woman's positive description of the man (5:10–16), but the real meeting hasn't happened. We probably all know people who are genuine 'admirers' of God, yet seem still to be one step removed from him, to have never quite connected.

From this point of view, the final verses (6:2–3) give hope. Although, somehow, the meeting never happened, the person didn't enter into a real relationship with God and the opportunity seems to have passed, in the end they belong to God and God to them. The fumbling failure is not permanent. Indeed, we could see the whole passage from the point of view of ourselves, in our failure to connect with God in our ongoing life. The failure is painful and frustrating, but in the end it doesn't change the fact that we are God's and God is ours.

3 Beauty and desire

Song of Songs 6:4—7:13

A new section begins. Now it is the man's voice that dominates, with two descriptions of the woman's beauty (6:4–9; 7:1–9), concluding with the woman's invitation to the man (7:11–13).

The description of the woman includes many terms already encountered. There are some new notes, though. Chapter 6:4–5 depicts her as majestic and powerful—even dangerous—like a city or army, and with eyes that overwhelm. Female beauty is not correlated to submissiveness or passivity here. Verses 6–10 emphasise her beauty by comparison with others: even in a king's harem she would stand out. An unclear word appears in 7:2. The word translated here as 'navel' is perhaps better translated 'valley', with a clear sexual meaning, given that it occurs in sequence between her thighs and her belly. We could also see double meaning in the word 'mixed' as something that her 'valley' will not lack, for while it certainly can mean 'mixed wine' (Psalm 75:8) it could also refer to the mingled juices of the lovers.

Chapter 6:11–13 is also difficult to translate. Here we seem to swap to the woman's voice, as she recalls her desire for the man—perhaps suggesting that he was her 'first love' (the vines were just starting to bud). She is described as a Shulammite, but scholars have no clear sense of what this means, nor what a 'dance before two armies' is. Nevertheless, we get the idea that it was 'love at first sight' for her, and that her beauty caused heads to turn (v. 13).

The reference to 'desire' in 7:10 has intriguing echoes, for the word appears elsewhere only in Genesis 3:16 and 4:7. In 3:16, the woman is told that because of humanity's sin, 'your desire shall be for your husband, and he shall rule over you'. Here in the Song, it is the man who has 'desire' for the woman and the woman is inviting the man; there is no 'rule' over her (indeed, remember the image of the 'powerful' woman in 6:4–5). Perhaps we should see in this the hint that the inequality ('desire' and 'rule') that sin produces between the sexes can be resolved in true love. The same hint is in the Anglican marriage service, which speaks of marriage as God's gift through which man and woman 'may know the grace of God' (grace being the reversal of sin's effect) and may 'grow to maturity in love' (the goal of our discipleship: Ephesians 4:13).

Physical beauty and sexual desire are to be celebrated, not feared. Indeed, there is a hint that in the willing emotional and sexual union of the man and the woman, something powerfully good is present.

4 Beauty and desire

Song of Songs 6:4—7:13

Once again we are faced with the challenge of reading about passion and desire, not from us to God but from God to us. We read his praise of our beauty, although presumably, as we move from the literal talk of a man and woman to a spiritual interpretation, we should also broaden the sense of what is being praised—not so much our physical appearance as our essence, 'who we really are'. Perhaps this praise shouldn't surprise us: after all, God created us and uniquely pronounced humanity 'very good' (Genesis 1:31; compared with the mere 'good' he uttered about the sun, stars, plants and animals: vv. 4, 10, 12, 18, 21, 25).

God's desire is for us (7:10). This is a shocking statement, but it sits at the heart of the Christian faith: 'For God so loved the world that he gave his only Son' (John 3:16); 'God proves his love for us in that while we still were sinners Christ died for us' (Romans 5:8); 'He who did not withhold his own Son, but gave him up for all of us, will he not with him also give us everything else?' (Romans 8:32). Perhaps we think of this too easily as some generalised truth about God—'this is the sort of thing God does'—and lose the sense that God's sacrifice was powered by his desire, his longing, for us. We can also begin to grasp something of God's pain when we turn away from him and reject his love. The Song pushes us to think that God would not just be sad but 'broken-hearted'.

We can also usefully compare our response to God with the woman's in 7:11–13. Is God 'our beloved'? We can all understand the passion and exclusivity in the declaration 'I am my beloved's' (v. 10); is this the measure of our commitment to God? In the context of physical love, we recognise the importance of the woman's invitation and offering of herself to the man (vv. 12–14). We know that it is possible for a man to force himself on a woman, and so we put great importance on invitation and consent. They are what distinguish loving sex (a highpoint in human emotion and experience) from rape (a truly evil act). Yet bizarrely we sometimes seem to wish that God would just 'overpower us', 'intervene and turn us around', 'blast us with a sign from the sky'. The woman's invitation here reminds us that God waits to be invited.

5 The value of love

Song of Songs 8

In this final chapter, we leave fantasy behind and come back to earth with the reality of the clash of desire, love and social customs. What emerges is a shockingly modern-seeming emphasis on love above all things.

In verses 1–3 we find the woman dreaming, longing for her man (compare 3:1–5). In her earlier fantasy, her longing found fulfilment, but now it is bound in by what people will think (v. 1). Her wish is to bring him home to her mother—a rather more moderate and socially acceptable desire than a night of passion in the vineyards (7:13). Then we hear again the plea not to 'stir up or awaken love until it is ready'. Her longing, when it cannot be fulfilled, only causes her heartache. In her fantasy elsewhere in the Song, desire finds wonderful fulfilment. In the real world it is not so easy, and so we are advised not to awaken unfulfillable desire.

Nobody really understands verse 5b. Perhaps it hints at the 'cycle of life', if we follow the NIV translation: 'Under the apple tree I roused you; there your mother conceived you, there she who was in labour gave you birth'. Women conceiving and giving birth—both acts of love—make the world go round. This connects with the great praise of love in verses 6–7. Love chases us with the same passion as the one thing we can't escape (death and the grave). Fire and water are powerful natural images, but they may point to something more. 'Raging fire' could be translated as 'flames of Yahweh', the very fire of God. 'Many waters' points to the primeval chaos from which God created the world (Genesis 1:3). Love is the power of God; love can carve out order and beauty from chaos.

Verses 7b–12 are best taken as a rejection of love as a commodity, something that we, or our social customs, put a price on. Verses 8–9 depict the mentality of a woman's brothers (and other male relatives) in many societies, seeing it as their role to 'protect their sister's honour' (compare 1:6). She asserts her independence (v. 10)—to be a wall if she wishes, and to be his if she wishes. The man replies that King Solomon may have had many women (6:8–9: good for him!) but this woman is his own and that is all that matters (vv. 11–12). In fact, these verses could just as well be spoken by the woman, for she speaks of her own vineyard in 1:6 and this would continue the theme of her independence. Perhaps it is fitting that, at the end of the Song, the same words could be said by either lover, as they celebrate the unsurpassed value of their love.

6 The greatest of these is love

As we reach this final chapter of the Song, the boundary between a literal and spiritual interpretation starts to waver, as the literal becomes a reflection on the value and power of love. Love is the greatest power in the universe, the Song claims (vv. 6–7). This comes close to Paul's famous words: 'If I speak in the tongues of mortals and of angels… if I have prophetic powers, and understand all mysteries and all knowledge, and if I have all faith, so as to remove mountains… If I give away all my possessions, and if I hand over my body so that I may boast, but do not have love, I gain nothing… Love … bears all things, believes all things, hopes all things, endures all things. Love never ends… Now faith, hope, and love abide, these three; and the greatest of these is love' (1 Corinthians 13:1–3, 7–8, 13).

Paul's words are about 'love', just as the Song is literally about love. But the setting in 1 Corinthians makes clear that this 'love' is a spiritual gift from God (12:31, 14:1). Our love for others is in some way a reflection of, and an overflow from, our love for God and his love for us. Or, to quote John, 'God is love, and those who abide in love abide in God, and God abides in them' (1 John 4:16).

It is easy to miss the importance of this, as if it is a truism, so obvious as to be valueless. But many people do not see 'love' as the strongest power in the universe, nor the longing and passion between lovers as the clearest pointer to the perfect relationship between God and people. Many might see rational, impartial 'justice' as a more important core quality for God than emotional, driven 'love', but Jesus and the prophets before him seemed to challenge this view. For example, Hosea 6:6, 'For I desire steadfast love and not sacrifice', is echoed in Matthew 9:13; 12:7; Jesus instructs us to love even our enemies (5:43–45); there is a continued stress in Jesus' ministry on his compassion and love for those he meets (9:36); he sums up the law as love for God and neighbour (Mark

12:29–34). Peter even wrote, 'Love covers a multitude of sins' (1 Peter 4:8).

Love, the Song of Songs asserts, freely given and received between one man and one woman, is of immense power. It is this love that points us most clearly to the true relationship between God and humankind.

Guidelines

If the Song of Songs is right, and love is the strongest power in the universe, what might that mean for the way we act? The Song points to the freely given and received love between one man and one woman as the closest parallel for the true relationship between God and us, between God and you. It's intriguing. Many of us, if asked to think of the strongest love, might say the love between a mother and her child. Perhaps, but that is non-symmetrical: there may be love between child and mother and between mother and child, but they are not the same sort of love. It is the symmetrical love between lovers that the Song holds out to us. How would we cultivate that?

For many of us, the first difficulty is believing that God really does think we are beautiful and that he is passionate about us. Equally, though, for much of the time we treat God with a casualness that, if translated into a relationship with a human lover, would obviously bring the relationship to a bad end.

As we finish our readings in the Song of Songs, it is worthwhile pondering whether we place enough value on 'love' as a motivating power— as a guide and dynamic for action—and what changes might come if we were to model our relationship with God on a relationship with a husband or wife.

The cross

The cross is one of the most stark and uncomfortable aspects of Christian belief. This image of suffering and death at the heart of our faith is one that seems odd, even offensive. The early Christians faced exactly this charge, that it was nonsensical to see the death of a criminal crucified outside the walls of Jerusalem as the turning point of history. Yet they held to the belief that the cross is a vital clue to wisdom. Over the next two weeks, we will be looking at aspects of the cross.

The first week looks mainly at 1 Corinthians 1—2, a passage where Paul discusses the paradox of the cross and all that it means for Christian life. The second week looks at a series of other passages in the New Testament where, like a diamond, the cross is held up from different angles to show its rich and profound significance and to demonstrate how it changes the world.

Quotations are taken from Today's New International Version of the Bible.

22–28 October

1   The cross and wisdom

1 Corinthians 1:18–25

In Corinth, Paul faced a version of wisdom. The kind highly prized in this Greek city was primarily that of the Greek philosophers and teachers, known for their intellectual prowess and rhetorical skill. People in the church at Corinth were evidently impressed by such 'wise and persuasive words' (2:4).

Yet Paul stands before them armed with a message that centres on a crucified Jewish manual labourer. He reminds them, and us, that at the heart of Christian proclamation lies the cross—a form of death reserved for runaway slaves, condemned murderers and political rebels, people so foolish that you needed to make a public example of them.

If you ended up crucified, you had clearly done something wrong or were simply too stupid to get out of the way. Yet Christian faith points to this crucified man as the salvation of the world. This is God saving the world from itself. *This* is where truth and wisdom are found—in a convicted, crucified criminal hanging on a cross. It sounds ridiculous, confounding all common sense and wisdom.

We still don't understand it today. The cross, this scene of violence and pain, is something we want to run from, not embrace. Yet, as Martin Luther's mentor Johann von Staupitz said to him once, 'If you want to understand the Christian God, start with the wounds of Christ.'

I once bought a book of essays entitled *The God I Want*. We can't have it that way. If we use our own ideas of what God might be like or should be like, we end up making gods in our own image, gods who never challenge us and therefore cannot save us.

When we start trying to understand God, we have to start all over again. We have to give up human wisdom and learn God's new wisdom. This doesn't mean giving up thinking—far from it—but it does mean learning to think new thoughts in new ways. There is a logic, a rationality, to Christian faith, but it is one that starts at the cross.

The message of the cross will always seem like foolishness to some. Yet the cross is where we must begin if we are to understand this surprising and unexpected God.

2 The cross and power

1 Corinthians 1:26–31

In the young church at Corinth, it seems that much of the trouble (and there was quite a bit, reading between the lines) came from a wealthy, powerful group, perhaps fans of the rhetorically impressive Apollos (1:12; 3:5–6). They kept their distance from the poorer, less prestigious members of the church. They enjoyed dinner parties in pagan temples with their wealthy friends, eating meat that had been used in pagan sacrifice, regardless of the scruples of poorer Christians who not only were shocked by the scandal of eating in such an unholy place but also associated meat with the only time they could ever afford to eat it—when it was offered free at pagan festivals. When it came to the Christian meal, the *agape* supper, the beautiful people ate separately, perhaps even with better quality food and fine wines (11:21–22). These people understood how power confers privilege and privacy. At least, that is the way it works in the world, but not in the kingdom of God.

Against all this, Paul points out the awkward truth that most of the Corinthian church members were pretty ordinary. Just as God chose to save the world through an event that seemed to mean nothing—just another Roman crucifixion of a criminal—he has also chosen a group of (mostly) nonentities as his representatives in Corinth. If it were me, I would have chosen the bright, the beautiful, those with influence. It seems that God, by and large, doesn't. Just as God chose to save the world through a powerless, crucified man, so he chose the weak and unimpressive for his purposes in Corinth.

Why? The answer comes in verse 29: 'so that no one may boast before him'. Our constant tendency is to boast of our own career, looks, achievements and talents, which give us the power to get what we want. We think that these qualities are what count.

Yet a moment's reflection reminds us that these things are all temporary. We lose jobs; looks fade; achievements seem less impressive with time; talents are overtaken by other, greater talents. The cross teaches us God's way—to learn not to boast in anything as insubstantial as social status, political power or human achievement, but to 'let those who boast boast in the Lord' (v. 30).

God sometimes has to take away the things we are tempted to boast in, so that we can learn to boast in him. He breaks up shaky foundations to build stronger ones. Only when we learn to find our greatest delight and comfort not in our own achievements, gifts or status, but in the love that took Christ to the cross, can we find true security.

3 The cross and weakness

1 Corinthians 2:1–5

Paul reminds the Corinthians that when he first came to them, he cut a pretty sorry figure. He was clearly suffering from some kind of illness, which elsewhere he calls his 'thorn in the flesh'—perhaps a persistent eye condition. It also seems that he was not a particularly impressive speaker, especially compared with the talented Apollos. This was Paul, the man who was known to send people to sleep while he was speaking (Acts 20:9) and who called himself an 'idiot' when it came to rhetoric (2 Corinthians 11:6, literally).

Clearly, however, Paul doesn't try to hide this experience of weakness. Instead, he boasts of it: 'If I must boast, I will boast of the things that show my weakness' (2 Corinthians 11:30). The reason he does this is surely that he has understood something of the way God works, which is revealed in the cross. How does God achieve the most difficult task of all—the salvation of the world? He does it through a cross, by a display of weakness and powerlessness. If ever there was a picture of weakness, it is a crucifixion—a person pinned to a plank of wood, unable to move, even to breathe. God achieved salvation through the weakness of the cross. Perhaps he can do more through our weaknesses than our strengths.

The experience of weakness and failure can be the beginning of wisdom. When we fail, or when our bodies fail us, it is not that God learns something new about us. He knows our weakness long before we do. It might well be, however, that we learn something new about ourselves. Failure and weakness, when we come face to face with our limitations, can help us realise that we are not the people we thought we were. We are not immortal; we are not infallible. We are not God.

If it is true that what we are is more important than what we do (because what we do comes out of what we are), then the experience of our own weakness can bring about qualities of humility, generosity to others, the kindness that comes from sympathy, grace and gentleness with others' failings. Success can easily make us proud, arrogant, patronising and dismissive.

If you think you have failed as a Christian, join the club. God loves you and sent his Son for you, not because you are a good Christian but because you are a bad one. We are invited to get to know the God who loves the weak and the failing, who often works precisely through weakness and failure, who can turn those very things into his means of blessing us and, through us, his world.

4 The cross and mystery

1 Corinthians 2:6–11

Jesus died alone, abandoned by his friends and supporters and even, it seems, by God. The cry 'My God, my God, why have you forsaken me?' (Matthew 27:46) is the most heart-rending cry in all of scripture. Even then it was misunderstood. The crowd thought he was calling for Elijah (v. 49). The Romans perhaps thought he was just another sufferer who had lost his faith.

We, too, struggle to understand. Why did Jesus have to die? We need to try to understand, because, as Anselm reminds us, faith always seeks understanding. At the heart of the universe is a God who is the source of life, love and beauty. Yet the relationship between him and us, his creation, has been fractured. Deep wrong and severe pain between friends or partners cannot be glossed over if real reconciliation is to take place. Trivial offences can be excused, but excusing is different from forgiving. Excusing is easy: there is nothing to forgive. Real forgiveness always costs. It is difficult, costly, painful, hard. Suffering is always at the heart of forgiveness.

Jesus, in some way, dies in our place. He takes our sin upon himself. What that meant for him, we can barely imagine. The Gospels give us little explanation of the meaning of the death of Jesus. They simply tell the story, giving hints but little sustained reflection. In the rest of the New Testament, different images are used—a law court, a ransom, the reconciliation of friends, sacrifice in the Jerusalem temple—but these are metaphors, not final meanings. They help us understand a little of why the cross was necessary or how it all worked, but they never exhaust its meaning. Jesus is abandoned by God so that we might never be. However we explain it, though, there remains an element of mystery about the death of Christ, something we can never entirely fathom, because it speaks of 'what no eye has seen, what no ear has heard, and what no human mind has conceived' (v. 9).

Before the cross, ultimately, we can only worship. At the end of the day, our theologies, theories and models of the atonement, important and useful as they are, fall silent. You cannot give a lecture at the foot of the cross. Like the centurion, we can only wonder: 'Surely he was the Son of God!' (Matthew 27:54).

5 The cross and the Spirit

1 Corinthians 2:10–16

Paul's rumination on the cross leads him to thinking of the Spirit, who 'searches all things, even the deep things of God' (v. 10). It leads him particularly to the climax of the chapter, the deceptively simple statement, 'But we have the mind of Christ.'

Paul draws a contrast between the spirit of the world and the Holy Spirit, the Spirit who is from God (v. 12). The contrast is between the 'spirit of the age'—the normal way of thinking, living and acting in any given culture—and the Holy Spirit, who enables us to speak a different language: 'words taught by the Spirit, explaining spiritual realities with Spirit-taught words' (v. 13). This might be understood literally, as a reference to the gift of tongues, a spiritual language that goes beyond normal rational processes to express the heart's desire to God. Or it might refer to a different viewpoint, the new way of looking at the world, when it is seen from the cross. The 'words taught by the Spirit' are perhaps best understood as referring to both—tongues being a sign or picture of this different rationality, this alternative way of reading the world.

This is still a reflection on the cross. As we have seen, the cross teaches a different wisdom, and so the true sign of the presence of the Spirit is to have the mind of Christ, the crucified Christ. It is the mind, the attitude, that not only prays but constantly thinks, 'Thy kingdom come'. It is set not on money, fame, sex and power but on love, joy, peace, patience, goodness, kindness, gentleness, faithfulness and self-control (Galatians 5:22–23). It is constantly thinking about what will advance God's kingdom, and includes the willingness to do whatever it takes to see that happen, even if it leads to something like a cross.

To have the Spirit is to begin to 'know the thoughts of God' (v. 11). It is to begin thinking as God does, not as humans tend to do. If this seems impossible… exactly! It is—or, at least, it would be without the gift of the Spirit, for whom we must learn to pray daily: 'Come, Holy Spirit.'

6 The cross and love

1 Corinthians 13:1–3

It is always tempting to think that if we love God enough, he will love us in return. If we say our prayers, go to church, be as good a Christian as we can and stay out of trouble, then God will make sure things go well for us. This is religion as a contract, a deal struck between us and God: we shake hands and expect him to keep his side of the bargain.

Yet it doesn't work that way with God. In Christian faith, it is God's love that triggers ours, not the other way round. We do not make God love us by our devotion; his love comes first. In a healthy family, a child who knows he is loved grows up with the ability and the security to love others. In an unhealthy family, where its members only receive love when they succeed or behave as they are supposed to, children learn to treat others in that same reserved, conditional way.

When we contemplate the cross, its central message is that of love: as John put it, 'This is love: not that we loved God, but that he loved us and sent his Son as an atoning sacrifice for our sins' (1 John 4:10). The cross is a picture of how far God will go to redeem his broken creation, which includes you and me. It is a picture of how much we are worth to God—which means that it shows how much we are worth, full stop.

The central character in Victor Hugo's novel *Les Misérables* is Jean Valjean, a criminal on the run. He steals a bishop's silver candlesticks and is arrested. To his surprise, the bishop not only refuses to accuse him; he also gives him his remaining candlesticks. Instead of the years of prison that he deserved, he walks free. It is an act of transforming grace, which has a dramatic effect on Valjean. It turns him from a self-seeking scoundrel to a man bent on generosity and kindness, one of the greatest pictures of goodness in European literature.

Grace, forgiveness and love are the most powerful forces in the world. Love can warm hearts, change minds and bend wills. The cross has power because it is an ultimate act of love, the act of a God who loved the world so much that he gave his only Son.

The person described in 1 Corinthians 13 is a person who has understood the cross. He or she has learnt to live a life dominated not by the will to succeed, to gain comfort or prosperity, but by the will to love, knowing that far more is achieved by love than by anything else.

How do we respond to the love that God demonstrates at the cross? By learning to live in that love and turning it into small but real acts of love for others. Think of the people you might meet today and of the small but significant ways in which you can show them the costly love of Christ.

Guidelines

The cross invites us to think differently, to turn our values upside down. It teaches us to look at our failures not as disasters but opportunities to grow. It teaches us to value the weaker, less impressive members of our churches, looking for what we can learn from those who we least expect to teach us anything. It teaches us to love as God has loved us. As you reflect on this week's readings, why not think on and pray through the following:

- Are there simple ways in which you can show love that costs you something to those who cross your path regularly?
- What do you normally 'boast in'? What do you rely on to make yourself feel good about yourself?
- Identify the people you tend to dismiss as insignificant, and ponder what they might have to teach you.

29 October–4 November

1 Peace through his blood

Colossians 1:15–23

Ian McEwan's book *Atonement* (Vintage, 2005) tells the story of a young girl, Briony Tallis, who mistakenly accuses her sister's boyfriend of rape. He is sent to jail and his life is ruined. The book is about her guilt and her desperate attempts to atone for what she has done. She needs somehow to find atonement, or forgiveness. The tragedy of the book is that she doesn't find it. Towards the end, we read this: 'All she wanted to do was work, then bathe and sleep until it was time to work again. But it was all useless, she knew. Whatever... she did, and however well or hard she did it… she would never undo the damage. She was unforgivable' (p. 285).

Christian theology says that each broken relationship, each act of disdain, each tragic life wasted is a symptom of something much deeper—a wound that lies at the very heart of creation. John Henry Newman wrote, 'We live in a world which is out of joint with the purposes of its creator.' You cannot just ignore it when something has gone deeply wrong. Something needs to be done to make it right. Atonement needs to be made.

Today's reading from Colossians tells of that deep wound in creation, which can only be healed through atonement, mysteriously provided for us in the death of Christ: 'peace through his blood, shed on the cross' (v. 20). God, our Creator, has provided atonement through the death of his Son, Jesus, who died both as the divine Son of God and as one of us, a human being taking the sins of others on his shoulders. Because of the cross, we now live in a world where atonement has been made. The tragedy of this world has been atoned for. We live in a world that has been forgiven.

Many people go through life making one of two very common mistakes, either thinking they don't need forgiveness or thinking they never can be forgiven. Truth and reality dawn when we realise that neither of these beliefs is true. Back in the 1970s, there were occasional news stories of isolated Japanese soldiers still defending a Pacific island, thinking that World War II was still going on. It hadn't dawned on them that, actually, everything had changed. The war was over. There was now a new world. Because of the cross, we too live in a new world, a world that still hurts from the pain of sin and evil, but a world where that sin is atoned for, a world that now awaits its final liberation.

2 Come down from the cross and save yourself!

Mark 15:21–32

One of the strangest parts of the Good Friday story is the mocking accusation hurled by the people around the cross: 'He saved others, but he can't save himself!' (v. 31). As a performer of miracles, Jesus is presumably perfectly capable of coming down from the cross. What better proof could there be that he is the divine Son of God than his miraculously coming down from the cross where he has been nailed by Roman soldiers? But he doesn't. Why not?

Imagine for a moment that Jesus had come down from the cross. Imagine that, as he hangs there, suddenly a crowd of angels comes down, the nails spring out, the wounds heal over and he climbs down from the cross, wandering off into the sunset, followed by his disciples, to live happily ever after.

What would it have been like for us if that had happened? There will come a day when you and I face death for ourselves, and at that moment we will pray that somehow God will be with us as we face this final journey. Imagine, at that moment, having to reflect that Jesus ducked out and escaped death. He didn't go through with it. Imagine that the God we pray to doesn't know what it's like to die, and that, when we face that day, we're on our own.

There may come a day that you're aware that your friends failed to stand by you when you needed them, and you wonder whether God will do the same. Would he really go the extra mile for you? Does he really care about you? Imagine having to think again, at that moment, that Jesus didn't quite get there. He didn't go through with it. He chose to impress the crowd rather than embrace death for you.

Of course, the truth is that Jesus did go through with the cross—which means that when you and I face the worst experiences of our lives, when you and I face the day of our death, we can know that God has been there first. He has blazed the trail and we just follow in his footsteps. As a result of that, we need fear nothing. The Scottish theologian John MacMurray once wrote this:

The maxim of illusory religion runs: 'Fear not; trust in God and he will see that none of the things you fear will happen to you'; that of real religion, on the contrary, is this: 'Fear not; the things that you are afraid of may well happen to you, but they are nothing to be afraid of.'
QUOTED IN MICHAEL MAYNE, YEAR LOST AND FOUND (DLT, 1987)

3 Crucified with Christ

Galatians 2:17–21

The question of identity is one of the deepest human questions. In this passage, Paul writes of how he has been 'crucified with Christ': his old 'self' has died and a new one has been born. Those whose faith is in Christ are new people. It is not just that they *should be* new people, but that they *are* new people. This is symbolised in infant baptism, where we are given a Christian name—not just our family name that we've inherited and didn't really have any choice over, but an individual name that gives us a new identity, a new identity in Christ.

The old 'Paul' was proud of his ancestry and full of animosity towards people who were different from him. But when Christ came to him, it was as if that person died and a new person was born. For him, the new birth actually was embodied in a new name. He changed from Saul of Tarsus to Paul the Christian—a new person, forgiven, free, and oriented entirely towards the Son of God 'who loved me and gave himself for me' (v. 20).

Occasionally we hear of a witness to a crime, or a juvenile offender, who is given a new identity, a new name, a new location, a new role. No one knows who they are. They start again. That person's task is to learn to live out of the new identity they've been given as if they really are a new person, with everything new. That can be difficult, as many psychological studies suggest. There is still the 'pull' of the old self, the old habits, the old name and the old ways of life.

If the cross of Christ is to benefit us, it must mean a death not just for him but, in a way, for us as well. It means that our old selves die. The old self, defined primarily by family, social status, ethnic origin, gender and sexuality—maybe past sins, mistakes and failures, or even achievements and prizes—dies, and a new person is born, our new Christian self.

That is what it means to be 'crucified with Christ'—to live as new people, defined not by the past but by the future. Our identity is defined not by what we have been but by what we will one day become: restored, redeemed, forgiven in Christ.

4 Becoming like him in his death

George MacDonald once wrote, 'Christ died to save us, not from suffering, but from ourselves. Not from injustice, but from being unjust. He died that we might live, but to live as he lives, by dying as he died, who died to self' (C.S. Lewis, *George MacDonald: An Anthology* (Geoffrey Bles, 1946).

The destiny of everyone on the path of Christian life is to become like Jesus. We are perhaps familiar with the idea of the Christian life as 'becoming more like Jesus', but this passage from Philippians talks soberly of 'becoming like him in his death' (v. 10). If we really want to become like Jesus, it will cost us.

Why might it cost us to become like Jesus? Becoming like Jesus means becoming like God, because he is 'the image of the invisible God' (Colossians 1:15). If we ask the question, 'What is God like?' there is one simple answer: he is pure love. Love, of course, is not a feeling; it's about having a certain direction, a certain orientation towards people that issues in action. It's a kind of self-giving. The cross is perhaps one of the most perfect revelations of the nature of God, because it is God giving himself for us, giving himself for the life of the world. And so, if we are to become like Jesus, like God, it means that we need to learn to love, to learn to give ourselves. It means learning to die just a little bit to the old way of life that is all about me and my will and my comfort and my pleasures, and learning instead to live a life that is centred upon my relationships with people around me, the people whom God calls me to love. That is what we were made for—to become like Jesus, to learn to love, even when it hurts.

The problem is that we get rather comfortable with what we are, and we settle for it. There's a moment in the Disney film *The Lion King* where the lion cub who thinks he is guilty of the death of his father runs away into the jungle and starts wasting his life with a meerkat and a warthog. At one point, he has a vision of his father, who says to him, 'Remember who you are. You are more than what you have become.' Through the cross, God says that to us: 'Remember who you are. You are more than what you have become.' You were made to be like God. You were made to be capable of endless love and the deep, deep joy that comes from it. Don't settle for anything less.

5 Life through the man Jesus Christ

2 Corinthians 4:7–12

We normally think that life ends in death. One day we will have to die. At the end of life we put bodies in the ground and they decay. We make things; they get broken; we throw them away or they rust. We're used to the idea that things exist, they live, then they die and that's it. Life ends in death.

Because of the cross of Jesus, however, we Christians beg to differ. We don't believe that life ends in death, or at least it doesn't have to. Christians have always said that it's not that life ends in death, but that death leads to life. In our passage today, Paul says, 'We always carry around in our body the death of Jesus, so that the life of Jesus may also be revealed in our body' (v. 10). His experience as an apostle often felt like death. He was kicked around the Mediterranean, contradicted, misunderstood and shipwrecked. His body was not what it used to be: it was, as he puts it, 'wasting away' (4:16). You get up early to pray day after day when you'd much rather stay in bed. You keep ringing up that depressed friend, even though you don't look forward to the conversation. You keep trying to treat that difficult colleague with something approaching love, even though their arrogance is really hard to bear. You keep trusting God and believing that he is in control when it doesn't feel as if he is. Sometimes it all feels a bit like death.

Yet Paul also recognises something else happening in him. It is not just the death of Jesus that is being carried around in his body; somehow, the life of Jesus is also being made manifest. There is a silent change taking place inside him: he is being renewed within. Maybe you notice, over time, that your tastes begin to change. The desire to gossip or to cling on to what's your own, or the tendency to get angry, fades just a little bit as each year goes by. In its place you find something of a hunger for God arising within you; a desire for the humility and generosity of Christ begins to take root.

In a mysterious way, our response to the cross of Christ is to re-enact the same pattern in our lives. Through a life of self-giving, a life of love, which can often feel like a kind of death, God brings life both to us and to the people around us.

6 For the joy set before him

Hebrews 12:1–11

There's a nagging question at the end of the story of the crucifixion: how did Jesus manage to endure the intense physical and spiritual agony of the cross? This reading from Hebrews gives us something of an answer: 'For the joy that was set before him he endured the cross, scorning its shame' (v. 2). Jesus went through this experience not because suffering was good for him but because joy was at the other end. Jesus mounted the cross not because pain would purify him but because it was the only way in which the world could be redeemed.

One of the Greek philosophies current at the time of Jesus was Stoicism. Stoics were, and still are, people who attach great importance to endurance. They have a deterministic view of the world, believing that things are just the way they are, and there's not much we can do about it. The world is often unfair but we simply have to attune ourselves to it. Then we become immune to misfortune, immune to suffering. Stoics value self-control because, if we can't do anything about the world, all we can control is ourselves.

Christians are different. Christians believe that the world is ultimately good, that justice and goodness win in the end. The final word is not suffering but joy, and so, in a sense, Christians never get used to suffering. It always feels wrong. We always pray and fight against it, especially the sufferings of others. That is the final call of the cross—for us to fight with Jesus through and against the suffering of God's world. We do it not because suffering is good for us, and not because it's an inevitable part of the world, but because we know that on the other side of it is joy. The last word is not pain or suffering or endurance; it is life and freedom and fulfilment.

Sometimes the world, or our own lives, can seem very dark and bleak.

At those moments, the Stoic thinks, 'You just have to get used to the darkness. That's all there is. Live with it.' Christians look out at the darkness and start to sing, because they know that even though it's night, day follows night: the dawn is coming. Pain and suffering are not illusory; they are real. But they are also temporary.

Guidelines

Some questions to ponder as we come to the end of this fortnight of considering the cross:

- We have been thinking this week that we live in a forgiven world. Yet we can so often, like the Japanese soldiers on the Pacific islands, continue to live as if this forgiveness does not apply to us. Is there something in your life today that you feel has never been quite forgiven? Might you confess it now and receive forgiveness from the cross, where your sin was atoned for?
- Where does your true identity lie? How would you answer the question 'Who am I?'
- As you reflect on suffering and pain in your life, where can you see God at work in it and where do you sense God calling you to pray and fight against it?
- Are there people in your networks or neighbourhood, or people in the wider world, whose suffering hurts you deeply? How might you join with God in struggling for life against the suffering of the world?

Psalms 89 (88)—100 (99)

It is high time we considered the titles of the Psalms. Many of the Psalms have a heading, usually printed in italics in our Bibles. These headings are not properly part of the psalms but were added later. Many of them are indications of the instruments to be used ('On oboe and harp' or 'For strings'), the chorus of singers for whom they were written or who were to sing them, or the type of psalm. One puzzling group provides the name of the tune ('To "The Doe of the Dawn"' or 'Lilies', or three consecutive psalms to 'Do not destroy'), just as, in modern hymn books, tunes have names such as 'Old Hundredth' or 'Helmsley'. These 'stage-directions' are straightforward enough.

A large group of the titles is attached to incidents in the life of David, inserted on the assumption that they were all composed by David. It is possible that some of the psalms were indeed composed by David; others were certainly not. One example of a psalm that is surely older than David's time is Psalm 29 (28), which was originally a Canaaanite hymn celebrating the lordship of Baal, adapted and adopted for the worship of Yahweh. An example of a psalm later than David is Psalm 51 (50). The title attaches it to David's repentance after his adultery with Bathsheba and his murder of her husband, Uriah. It is, of course, a psalm of repentance, but the final verse speaks of rebuilding the walls of Jerusalem, which dates it after the walls had been destroyed by the Babylonians. A psalm which it is attractive to attach to David is Psalm 110 (109); this, as we shall see, adopts the ritual of enthronement of a king of Jerusalem, and it could have been David's own enthronement.

These titles, then, may be helpful to the imagination, but are not safe guides to the composition or use of the psalms to which they are attached. This is all the more frustrating in that we have no clue as to how the psalms were gathered or how they were preserved or used. Some of them are obviously processional chants; some obviously have a repeated chorus-refrain (such as 'for his great love is without end'). But what of the highly individual laments or complaints in sickness or harassment? Did a faithful Israelite go into the temple, ask for a psalm useful for prayer in sickness or gratitude for deliverance, and receive a little prayer-card? We simply do not know.

1 I will sing for ever of your love, O Lord

Psalm 89 (88)

This psalm is at once both one of the most hopeful and one of the saddest of the psalms. It sets in contrast on the one hand God's love and fidelity and the promises announced to David, and on the other the failure of this promise. If God is loving and faithful, how can he have failed to fulfil his promise?

Seven times (the perfect number) in the course of the psalm, these two key qualities of God, love and faithfulness, are stressed in unison (vv. 1, 2, 14, 24, 28, 33, 49). *Hesed* is the indefectible family love which can be relied on above all things, especially in the close-knit Jewish family. The one rock of certainty is that home is always home and family will never let you down. This is God's love for his family. And *'emet*, God's truth and fidelity (improbably from the same root as the familiar word 'Amen'—but don't even think of trying to understand Hebrew roots!) means 'firmness' and 'security'. If God is not reliable, there is no such thing as reliability. These are the basic pillars of all certainty and security.

Add to these the covenant with David, an intensification of the covenant with Moses. In the story of King David, when David offered to build the temple as a house for the Lord, the Lord replied with a promise: David was not to build a house for the Lord, but the Lord would build a House for David—that is, a dynasty that would last for ever. Our psalm quotes this promise at length, and indeed this poetic version may well be older than the prose version given in 2 Samuel 7. The psalmist's problem is that, despite God's love and fidelity, the promise has not been kept: Israel has been dragged into exile, her king in chains and her monarchy shattered. Israel's consistent infidelity to the covenant, her flirting with other gods and her disregard of the poor, the weak and disadvantaged and all God's favourites, had left the Lord no alternative.

For the Christian, things look different. In the prologue to John's Gospel we are reminded that the law came through Moses, but grace and truth—the same words, *hesed* and *'emet*—through Jesus Christ. It is in

Christ that the promises of an eternal dynasty of the house of David are fulfilled. Do we turn our backs on this fulfilment just as determinedly as Israel turned her back on the covenant?

The psalm ends with a doxology, a couplet in praise of God. This is the ending not of this individual psalm, but of the third book of Psalms (compare Psalms 41 and 72).

2 You sweep men away like a dream!

Psalm 90 (89)

A meditation on time and eternity, this psalm sways between the stability of divine permanence and the instability of human life. Words for the passage of time abound: 'from age to age', 'a watch in the night', 'all our days', 'the span of our years', 'the number of our days', 'dawn' and 'the years when we looked upon evil'. All this reflection on the instability of human life contrasts with God's stability and the nearest approach to it that we know, the permanence of the mountains and the earth itself. In Palestine the grasses may be fresh and green in the morning but withered and brittle after a day scorched by the sun. In April the wild flowers and fruit-blossoms are brilliant; by the end of May all is yellow and cracked by the heat.

At the opening of the poem the author is keenly aware of the opening scenes of the Bible—creation and the Fall, with its penalty of death, the return to dust. The threefold mention of God's anger in verses 7–11 may give an impression that human instability is to be seen as a punishment for human sin, but there is much more emphasis on divine mercy, on wisdom of heart and on joy and success. These give the poem a mood of tranquillity and quiet rejoicing. There is no need to be afraid of the passage of time. The message is, then, perhaps one of contentment in the swirling changes and passage of human life, lived in the confidence of divine stability and divine care. All the circumstances of life may change but the Lord is still our refuge from generation to generation.

Seventy years, or 'eighty, if we are strong' (v. 10), was surely well over the expectancy of life in those days. Life was short and tough, with the ever-present threat of inexplicable and untreatable sickness, infertility, brigandage, injustice, famine and war. The immense ages ascribed by the Bible to the patriarchs of old are not to be taken literally. They are more signs of special divine blessing, enabling the founder figures to escape for a little longer the even grimmer fate of being simply dissolved back into the family stem. Nevertheless, the prayer ends in this psalm on the relaxed note of a double plea for success.

3 He who dwells in the shelter of the Most High

Psalm 91 (90)

For the Christian reader, the clue to the understanding of this psalm is given by its quotation by the Tempter ('Satan' means 'the Tempter' or 'Tester') in the story of Jesus' testing (Matthew 4:6). Jesus is in the desert after his baptism, working out what form his messianic mission should take. In the end, after the Tempter has put forward three false alternatives, Jesus sees that his mission is to be the suffering servant of the Lord. Meanwhile, however, three times the Tempter flaunts the scripture in front of Jesus, and each time Jesus replies with another text which shows that he has more control and understanding of the meaning of scripture than the Tester himself.

In the second test, the Tempter quotes sarcastically from today's psalm ('They shall bear you up on their hands lest you strike your foot against a stone') to voice the suggestion that Jesus thinks himself so close to God that he can come to no harm. Jesus replies with a quotation from Deuteronomy 6:16, 'You shall not put the Lord your God to the test.'

Yes, the Tester is right (there is always *some* attractive truth in the devil's suggestions) that the psalm meditates warmly and intimately on God's care and protection of one who puts full trust in the Most High. This is expressed in a lovely series of paired images running throughout the psalm as it details the dangers from which God will protect: the trickery of snares, fear of the dark, human violence, sickness, wild animals, and possibly a mythical dragon. Hebrew poetry in general, and the psalms in particular, derive their balance from such repetitious parallelism, but in this case the tranquillity imparted is especially satisfying: shelter and shade, refuge and stronghold, snare and plague, pinions and wings, buckler and shield, and so on. Occasionally there is an even closer, reversing link: clings in love – *free* – *protect* – knows my name (v. 14). In the monastic prayer of the Church, this psalm is prayed every evening at the final prayer of Compline, as the monk securely and contentedly yields himself into the care of God for the night.

4 It is good to give thanks to the Lord

Psalm 92 (91)

As explained in the introduction to these notes, the headings or titles that stand at the beginning of each psalm in the Bible were added later and are not part of the original psalms. At the head of this psalm stands a liturgical note: 'A song for the Sabbath'. It has been suggested that this ascription may come from the fact that the sacred name 'the Lord' occurs in the psalm seven times, the perfect number.

Whether or not this is the case, it is valuable to reflect on this mysterious name, which in Judaism is never pronounced. A superficial reason for this is that we do not know how it was pronounced. In classical Hebrew, only the consonants are written—in this case 'YHWH'. At one stage the word was turned into English as 'Jehovah', which is quite certainly incorrect. When the Four Letters occurred in the Hebrew text, the reader would read out 'Adonai', and eventually the vowels of 'Adonai' were married to the consonants of 'YHWH' to produce the misbegotten word 'Jehovah'.

The deeper reason, however, is that the name is both too intimate and too awesome to be spoken. It is not the common word for God or gods, but is the special name of the God of Israel. Each of us has a special, intimate family name, a term of endearment, often embarrassing but always a sign of deep love in the family and certainly not to be spoken to strangers. So YHWH lies too deep in the heart to be used aloud.

The word is also too awesome. It was revealed to Moses at the burning bush (Exodus 3:1–15). To reveal your name is a sign of friendship and trust. Once someone possesses your name, they can begin to unlock your secrets, to 'steal your identity'. The name was given to Moses as an assurance of God's patronage as he stood before Pharaoh, but no meaning was given on that occasion. When Moses asked the meaning, he was told merely 'I am who I am'. It was only later, when Israel had sinned and smashed the brand new alliance with God, that God revealed the meaning of the name. God passed before Moses, crying out, 'YHWH, YHWH, God of tenderness and compassion, slow to anger, rich in faithful love' (Exodus 34:6). This was the meaning and concept of their God which echoed down to the scriptures of Judaism—a God of loving forgiveness.

5 Greater than the roar of mighty waters

Psalm 93 (92)

This is the first of a group of psalms celebrating the kingship of the Lord, comprising also Psalms 95—99. Most of them include the refrain 'The Lord is King!' which can also be translated 'The Lord *has become* King'. For some years in the last century, it was strongly held that this cry indicated a festival celebrating the renewal of the kingship of the Lord. Such an annual festival existed in other Near Eastern countries, but it is difficult to believe that it was celebrated in Israel, since there is no explicit trace of it in the Bible and in the full instructions about festivals given there. It is also difficult to envisage, for Israel, the notion of God ever ceasing to be king, that his kingship should be renewed. In recent years the thesis has largely waned.

This psalm is among the oldest in the collection and probably dates from the very earliest times in Canaan. Baal, the chief Canaanite god, was a god of storm and the powers of nature, and the same imagery is applied here to the Lord. There is also the rhythm of early Canaanite poetry, most clearly visible in verse 3: one line of two elements, followed by a line in which a third is added: 'the rivers have lifted up, the rivers have lifted up their voice.'

In the early imagery of the Bible, water is rightly conceived as a mighty and terrifying force. As the chaos and death wreaked by a tsunami show, no natural weather phenomenon is as powerful. In addition, the Hebrew picture of primitive chaos is of a limitless mass of waters. God divides the waters to insert the world—a flat plate, covered by a dome, with sluice-gates in the dome to admit the rain—and then continues to hold back the waters. If, at any moment of his continuing act of creation, God were to withdraw this restraint on the waters, they would rush together again and the world would implode, leaving only the formless mass of waters.

A further element in the imagery is perhaps the sound-play of the central verses. Verse 3, about the rivers, is dominated by a gentle 'n' consonant, perhaps expressing the smooth-flowing waters, while verse 4, dominated by final -im, -am, -om, may render the booming of the waves of the sea. All of these seek to express the kingship of God over the natural forces of the world.

6   Avenging God, shine forth!

Psalm 94 (93)

The 'envelope' of this psalm, the first and last verses, concentrates on vengeance—not the most Christian of motifs. One of the great advances of Jesus' teaching in the Sermon on the Mount was the replacement of even the limited vengeance allowed by ancient law-codes and Mosaic legislation with the teaching on turning the other cheek. Within this envelope, however, comes a prayer of confidence that the Lord will not allow the persecution of those who trust in him to continue unheeded.

This provides us with a useful recognition of the universal human instinct of crying for vengeance. It cannot be disguised or neglected. Our automatic reaction to hurt is always to hurt back, to repay injury with injury, as though this promotes justice. Just as 'one good turn deserves another', so we assume that one bad turn deserves another. Does the principle of balance really apply in this case? Does the hurt inflicted in recompense for a hurt really restore a balance or merely provide a jumping-off point for a new spiral of injury? We can be misled by the image of the scales of justice, neatly balanced. The long-running individual and national feuds of history are enough to show that such a balance is no road to peace, whether the sphere is Northern Ireland, Israel, Rwanda or the long-running family feud. The spiral of tit-for-tat continues until the stronger of the two parties achieves the generosity of forgiveness. 'Blessed are the peacemakers' goes against every human instinct but, nevertheless, makes sense. Is it ever possible, though, without the strength that comes from God?

The other aspect of the psalm is confidence that God sees and pays heed to injustice. We cannot blind ourselves to the fact that injustice is done, but we can then turn to the Lord and accept that he who made the eye does indeed see, and invoke the mystery of suffering, again from the Beatitudes, 'Blessed are you when people persecute you on my account' (Matthew 5:11).

Guidelines

Particularly strong in the group of psalms that we have been considering is the emphasis on God's care for his people. So Psalm 90 starts off, 'O Lord, you have been our refuge'. Psalm 91 focuses on shelter in the Lord from all kinds of terrors. Psalm 92 dwells on the Lord as a picture of the wild ox's (in the Greek, the hippopotamus') strength for the young and the stability of age-old trees for the not-so-young. Psalm 93 offers the Lord as a stronghold, a rock of refuge. Especially in the exilic and post-exilic periods, when most of the psalms were composed, there is a craving for a personal relationship with God as a protection against the uncertainties of life. The old stabilities of kingship and temple had been shattered, and the little community that returned from Babylon to huddle round Jerusalem was surrounded by threats from enemies who resented their return, their rebuilding and their religious convictions.

If it is reasonable to say that we now live in a post-Christian world, much the same can be said in this day and age of the Christian. In many areas of the world, those who attempt to uphold Christian values are persecuted, even violently, by those of other religions or none, and by those who object to Christian championship of social values and concerns. Even within cultures that pay lip-service to Christian values, a Christian stance can often invite ridicule, contempt and opposition. Without a strong personal relationship with the Lord, supported by prayer and a conviction that the Lord is a stronghold for his own, the Christian can be lonely indeed. It is in such circumstances that these psalms may be especially helpful.

1 O that today you would listen to his voice

Psalm 95 (94)

The likeness of this psalm to Psalm 81 (80) is striking: both are divided into two parts, the first part being an invitation to come and worship, the second a reminiscence of the scenes of the exodus from Egypt and Israel's rebellions during that journey. It is almost as though both psalms were intended for the same liturgical shape of festival, although no festival is known which demands this style of liturgy.

The first seven verses constitute a call to approach for worship, bringing to mind the creative power of the Lord. These verses could form a processional song, leading up to an act of worship, kneeling in the temple. In many arrangements for monastic and other daily prayer, this psalm has indeed been used as the invitation to prayer at the beginning of the day.

The second half of the psalm harks back to a greater procession, the journey through the desert. It ends unsatisfactorily, as though cut short by God's oath that that generation would never enter his rest. However, a Christian view of these verses must be coloured by the use of the psalm in the letter to the Hebrews. Hebrews 4:1–11 links the divine mention of 'my rest' at the end of the psalm with the repose of God on the seventh day at the end of creation. This divine repose is seen as the goal of our journeying too, 'a seventh-day rest reserved for God's people'. 'Massah' (v. 8) means 'trial' or 'testing', and 'Meribah' means ' place of strife or judgment', for it was there that the people rebelled at the lack of water, until Moses appealed to God and struck the rock from which water flowed (Exodus 17:1–7). By their refusal to trust God, the people of the desert were denied the possibility of entering this rest. So God fixed a new 'today' to which Christians are still pressing forward on pilgrimage.

Christ, the supreme high priest, has already gone through to the highest heaven and Christians are to follow him in approaching the throne of grace to receive mercy and blessing. This theology of a journey is the foundation of the rich idea that the church is a pilgrim church, a church of sinners, still imperfect and still pressing forward to its goal. Each morning with this prayer the pilgrimage begins anew or takes one more step forward.

2 Sing a new song to the Lord

Psalm 96 (95)

It is possible to regard this psalm as having been artistically and artificially put together from a series of other psalms and hymns. Almost every line has its parallel elsewhere; details are given in the marginal references of some Bibles. This can be called the anthological style, as though flowers were picked from elsewhere and put together here to form a special bouquet. Then, again, it may all have been reused, for a very similar hymn is assigned to the Levites in the account of the transporting of the ark of the covenant to Jerusalem in 1 Chronicles 16:23–33. This suggests that the psalm was in use liturgically at the time when 1 Chronicles was written—that is, in the second century bc. This is, however, far from the suggestion that the psalm is secondary, let alone second-rate. It could also be that the author or authors used the common vocabulary of worship at the time.

In any case, the psalm carries two particularly strong impressions of Deutero-Isaiah, who prophesied in Babylon just before the end of the exile. One is the second stanza (vv. 4–6), which insists on strict monotheism, just as Deutero-Isaiah insistently maintains the purity of monotheism in the face of the many gods of Babylon (see, for example, Isaiah 44:6–20; 45:20–25). The other is the climax in the establishment of righteousness on earth, to which the final stanza leads (vv. 11–13), as does Isaiah 42:1–4. This 'righteousness' is sometimes translated as 'justice', but this is an impoverishment of the biblical concept. It is not justice in the sense of the treatment deserved by human, often sinful, action. God's righteousness is a saving justice. It does not consist in handing out due penalties and rewarding worthy behaviour. On the contrary, it is a forgiving justice that positively *makes* righteous any who turn to the Lord, and establishes peace and harmony on earth, despite human sin. As in verse 13, it is often allied to, and set in parallel with, God's truth, for in it God is being true to his promises, true to his nature as a forgiving God, fulfilling his covenant with Abraham and with his chosen people. So it is possible to pray, 'In your righteousness/justice set me free', not as a protestation of innocence but as an appeal for divine forgiveness. For Paul (in Romans 4), it is the righteousness given to Abraham not as a reward for any conduct of his own but simply because he trusted in God.

3 The Lord is king, let earth rejoice

Psalm 97 (96)

The prevailing imagery for the Lord in this psalm is light. There is a gradual progression. At the beginning we see only the sombre cloud and darkness around him, then a fire 'walks before him' (v. 3). His lightnings break forth to lighten the world. Their power is seen as the mountains melt like wax. Then (v. 6) the light spreads to the skies to proclaim his righteousness. The same imagery of light reappears in the final verses, as light shines forth for the righteous (v. 11).

In the Bible, light has always been a symbol of God, seen in the rainbow that symbolised God's renewed favour after the destruction brought by the flood, and in the lightning that showed God's presence on Mount Sinai, the brightness associated with the glory of God on the mountain and reflected on the face of Moses. Most of all, we see it in the brilliant light all round the figure in Ezekiel's vision of the glory of God's throne (Ezekiel 1:27–28).

Light, warmth and growth are associated with one another. The sun and light signify especially the beneficent presence of God, and nowhere more so than in Isaiah: a light shining in the darkness (9:2), or the eschatological splendour of Jerusalem in Isaiah 60, 'Arise, shine, for your light is come', where the light attracts the nations to the salvation offered to them at Jerusalem. In the New Testament, this imagery of light is transferred to Jesus: the glory of the Lord 'shines' round the shepherds at the birth of Jesus, and his garments are suffused with light at the transfiguration, signifying his divine state. So the Word incarnate is the light coming into the world (John 1:9), which some accept and some reject, and part of Jesus' divine claim is 'I am the light of the world' (John 8:12).

At the same time, the real glory of God, proclaimed by the skies (v. 6) is his righteousness, his saving justice which 'righteouses' sinners—that is, makes sinners righteous. This is the aspect of God's kingship celebrated in this psalm, that he brings sinners together in his kingdom of holiness and righteousness.

4 All the ends of the earth have seen salvation

Psalm 98 (97)

The striking feature of this psalm is its concern for the whole world. It shares with the psalms around it the same motifs of praise for the kingship of God, God's saving justice, his merciful family love for the house of Israel and his fidelity to his promises. The distinguishing feature, however, is the spread of all these qualities to the world as a whole. He has revealed his salvation in the sight of all nations (v. 2). All the ends of the earth have seen the salvation of our God (v. 3). All who dwell in the world acknowledge him (v. 7). He will judge the world and its peoples (v. 9). So often we think of Judaism as a closed religion, concerned with its own members' election as the chosen people and hostile to outsiders.

Jesus himself had little contact with non-Jews: in the Gospel of Mark we read of only one meeting with a Gentile, the Syro-Phoenician woman, whom he provokes to explicit faith by calling her a 'dog' (7:27). In John, the Gentiles make a roundabout approach to Jesus through one of the Twelve who happened to live on the borders of Galilee (John 12:20–21). At Pentecost there were present in Jerusalem representatives from all the nations around, but all were Jews. The events at Pentecost were followed by a great deal of hesitation over whether non-Jews could be received into the community of Christ's followers, and more hesitation about whether they must observe the Jewish law if they were received. Not until the letter to the Ephesians does the apostle teach that Christ has abolished the wall of separation to create in Christ a single new humanity from Jews and Gentiles (Ephesians 2:15).

It is almost as though a step backwards had been taken since the writing of our psalm, with its joyful celebration that 'all the ends of the earth' have seen the salvation of our God (v. 3)—the very expression used by the risen Lord to the apostles at the ascension. Yet from the exile onwards, the prophets are very conscious of the mission of Israel to bring salvation to the whole world. In dramatic contrast to the pre-exilic self-awareness of Israel and its separation from all other nations, the latest chapters of Isaiah are full of nations making their pilgrimage to Jerusalem to 'draw water from the springs of salvation' (12:3), sons and daughters coming from 'far away' to acknowledge the glory of the Lord (60:1–7). This was the beginning of the fulfilment of the promise to Abraham that all nations would bless themselves in his name.

5 The Lord is king; the peoples tremble

Psalm 99 (98)

It is not easy to discern the exact structure of this psalm, the last of this group of psalms celebrating the Lord as king. It falls into three sections, ending 'Holy is he' (v. 3), 'Holy is he' (v. 5), and 'Holy is the Lord our God' (v. 9) respectively. So it is basically about God as the holy king. Another emphasis in Hebrew is rather less obvious in English—the elevated position of God on high: 'God is exalted above all the peoples' (v. 2) and 'exalt the Lord our God' (vv. 5, 9), the same verb being used in each case.

This psalm is not about temporal dignity or worldly acclaim or power, but uniquely about that awesome, frightening but attractive quality of holiness. About this divine quality Augustine says, '*ardesco et inhorresco*', perhaps to be translated, 'I burn with ardour but I recoil in dread'. To the holiness of God any human being is inescapably drawn; yet so dauntingly far is it above our experience that we cannot but shrink away in awe. At his experience of it in the temple, the confident Isaiah could only shrink away in terror at his own uncleanness (6:5). In another poem (2:6-22) he cries out repeatedly, 'Go into the rock, hide in the dust, in terror of the Lord, at the brilliance of his majesty, when he arises to make the earth quake.'

The holiness of God is not something to be trifled with. Even as experienced—rarely—in holy people, it attracts and it daunts us as something wonderful, uncontrollable, beyond our ken and overwhelming. Moses was told, 'You cannot see God and live', and even what he did see of the glory of God left his face so calloused and scarred that he had to wear a veil (Exodus 34:35). In John, that was the daunting quality of Christ:

'We saw his glory, the glory that he has from the Father' (1:14), and at the marriage feast at Cana it is simply said, 'He revealed his glory, and his disciples believed in him' (2:11). In some way the glory of God was made visible, could be experienced, in Jesus.

This is the exaltation, beyond the level of this world, and the holiness of God which is celebrated in the kingship of God in this psalm.

6 'The Old Hundredth': a song of joyful praise

Psalm 100 (99)

Although there is no mention in this psalm of the kingship of Yahweh, it conveniently closes the series of psalms celebrating that kingship. It is the last of a group of psalms of pure praise—that is, not attached to any particular circumstances. All we can deduce is that the psalm was obviously designed to be sung at the approach and entry to the sanctuary, while the singers 'entered his gates with thanksgiving'. The initial 'Cry out' denotes a certain exaltation, a shout of triumph. The Hebrew word is used of sounding the trumpets for victory, as at the taking of Jericho by Joshua (Joshua 6:5, 10, 16, 20). However, we must remember that trumpets in those days were not our brass instruments; they were the much gentler rams' horns. So, at the coming of the humble king in Zechariah 9:9, the daughters of Jerusalem are bidden to rejoice with the same sound. In some Christian traditions, this psalm serves instead of the Benedictus as the final canticle of morning prayer, but it is also redolent with the quiet exaltation of spirit that Mary expresses in her Magnificat.

The psalm is rich in the favourite imagery of the psalmists, as valid for Christians as it was for the original authors:

- Universalism (v. 1): the call to praise is addressed to 'all the earth', not just to Israel. This suggests that the psalm was part of the liturgy of the second, post-exilic, temple.
- The Lord as the shepherd of his flock (v. 3).
- The two bases of our reliance on God (v. 5). However much we fail and 'mess up', once we have finally been convinced that we cannot rely on ourselves we can rely on God's *hesed*, his motherly or fatherly love, and his *'emunah*, his fidelity to his promises.

The middle line of verse 3 presents an interesting little problem: the same written Hebrew word can be read out with two different meanings, so that two translations are possible (just as, in English, the word 'read' can be either present or past, pronounced 'reed' or 'red')—either 'He made us and not we (ourselves)' or 'He made us and we (belong) to him'. The translators of the Old Testament into Greek chose the former version, and of course the Greek version rather than the Hebrew was the Bible used by the Church for the first four centuries. The later rabbinic tradition chose the latter. The written text must have been understood in both ways at different times and different places.

Guidelines

A special emphasis of this week's psalms has been on the kingship of God. When Samuel was judge in Israel, the people were ever more hindered and oppressed by the raids and invasions of the Philistines, their warlike neighbours on the Mediterranean coast. They felt that the needed a permanent military leader to repel the Philistines, and demanded of Samuel that he appoint them a king (1 Samuel 8:5). Samuel replied to them on two levels. They were not like other nations, he said, but the Lord was their king. Furthermore (the argument from self-interest), a king would be a heavy burden on them and would demand taxes from them in the form of labour. The Israelites were not to be diverted, however, and sadly Samuel reported the matter to the Lord. The Lord replied that they were to have their way (v. 22), but he still remained their king, as these prayers show.

In a democratic age, royalty may suggest only crowns, jewels and ceremony. In Israel it meant authority allied to responsibility. The people relied on their king for direction, protection, affection and care. In turn they owed their king loyalty and devotion. If this was the case with the human monarch, how much more was it true of the Lord as their king?

Above all, however, these prayers show that, despite the dynasty of human kings, the Lord is king on quite a different level. In the royal psalms, the qualities attributed to the Lord as king are transcendent ones—awe, majesty, glory. The king is to be approached with care and trembling, fear and reverence, as the Creator whose raiment is cloud and darkness, before whom the mountains melt like wax. This is why the Name is too holy to be pronounced, and why any attempt to make an image of the Lord is blasphemy.

Reflections of a pioneer

We live in an age of anxiety. There is regular press coverage about church decline. We sense the marginalisation of Christianity in our postmodern, post-Christendom culture and this feeds our sense of doom and gloom.

But is the tide turning? In some parts of the UK, churches are growing. Bishop Steve Croft coined the phrase 'Spring time in the church'. As Fresh Expressions team leader (for the Church of England and the Methodist Church) he travelled the country and noticed green shoots emerging where Christians had taken the initiative to plant churches for those who would not normally have any connection with church (see www.freshexpressions.org.uk). It was about taking seriously the call to 'proclaim the gospel afresh in every generation'.

We suffer from historical amnesia: there have always been generational changes. The Wesleyan revival exploited this fact as people moved from the country into towns like Bristol. (Imagine how gloomy those country parsons felt!) Who would have predicted Africa's growth from 5 million Christians in 1900 to 380 million in just 100 years? (But imagine how the Victorian missionaries felt, with so little to show for their efforts.) Our memory of church history is selective. We easily recall details of the Dark Ages but not the periods of great revivals and growth.

For these next two weeks, I have selected twelve passages that have particularly sustained me over the last six years as a Pioneer Minister. During this 'spring time' I was invited to plant a network church in Liverpool city centre for people in their 20s and 30s who are 'searching but don't get church'. I hope and pray that these reflections may also sustain and inspire you as you discern and follow God's calling to mission in the place where you find yourself.

All Bible quotations are from the New International Version of the Bible.

1 Jesus' compassion

Matthew 9:35–38

What is God's overriding sense when he looks at our society today? Does he stand in judgment on our materialistic society that is pillaging the world's resources? Is he angry that so many use his name as a swear word and choose to go their own way, or that our culture is so sexualised, or that nearly half of all marriages now end in divorce?

I believe that God's heart is expressed in Jesus' response to the crowds: 'He had *compassion* on them, because they were harassed and helpless, like sheep without a shepherd' (v. 36). The Greek word for 'compassion' here has a sense of 'gut-wrenching agony' about it (see also Mark 1:41). This is the same heartache that the father feels as he spots his prodigal son, still a long way off (Luke 15:20). As you think of the context where you live or work today, ask God for his heart for the people you know. So many in our culture are 'harassed and helpless', even if their troubles are well concealed behind a front that says, 'I'm in control, looking after number one.' When the curtain is drawn back, at the height of life's crises or joys, they know that they are sheep without a shepherd. 'The harvest is plentiful' is Jesus' diagnosis (v. 37). We would do well to take note.

What is Jesus' recommendation to us, his disciples? This is one of the few occasions in the Gospels when Jesus asks his disciples to pray for something specific (see also the garden of Gethsemane, Mark 14:38, and, regarding the end times, Matthew 24:20). Here they are to ask for God to send out workers. Jesus sees that the workers need to be sent out rather than waiting for customers to come to them.

Jesus often uses agricultural metaphors (such as the harvest) to describe his kingdom (see the parables in Mark 4 and Matthew 13). In our instant, 24/7 culture, this is a helpful reminder that things take time to grow and need space to be nurtured: there is no such thing as growth on demand. However, as any farmer will tell you, harvest time is a period of intense pressure, when the need to get out and bring in the crops before the autumn storms begin takes precedence over everything else. Then, there is an urgency about the work.

Is God calling you? Is there a place, person or situation that God has put on your heart? Talk to him about it, asking him to send out workers.

2   Jesus sends out the Seventy-two

Luke 10:1–12

Early in his ministry, Jesus selected the Twelve and then the Seventy-two. The first time the 'Seventy-two' get a mention, here in Luke 10, they are being 'sent out'. So what was Jesus' mission strategy?

He sent out workers 'two by two' (v. 1). If you sense a calling to go to people in your context, don't go it alone. Ask God for a partner or a small team. My experience is that if Superman/woman is in charge of the mission, this will be reflected in the culture of the church that is planted. God's Spirit has gifted us in different ways and we need each other (1 Corinthians 12). A team was the very first thing I prayed for in Liverpool when I was church planting from scratch. God very generously provided a marvellously gifted group of people who were a great blessing to me. I'm very glad I didn't try to start without them.

Again we read, 'The harvest is plentiful, but the workers are few' (v. 2). Farmers have to work hard—urgently—at harvest time to make sure all is 'safely gathered in'. Presuming Jesus' diagnosis is correct that the harvest is plentiful, a big reason why we don't see it is that we don't have enough workers (and this doesn't just mean vicars—even though the Church of England is desperately short of them at the moment). Like the foolish bridesmaids, we have become drowsy and fallen asleep (Matthew 25:3).

We are sent out 'like lambs among wolves' (v. 3). Mission is a war situation (2 Corinthians 10:4–5) so we can't expect an easy run. Jesus' life was in danger from the very start, from King Herod. Many Christians around the world live in danger of death, while, in the UK, we can be put off by the slightest media opposition. We should expect resistance.

'Do not take a purse or bag or sandals; and do not greet anyone on the road' (v. 4). Here is the sense of urgency again. How much time do we spend 'getting ready for mission'? We should travel light. 'The wind blows wherever it pleases' (John 3:8) so it is hard to plan ahead. Follow your instincts; make it up as you go along—like bringing up a child.

Find and *stay* with the 'man of peace' (v. 6). Not everyone will welcome you, but you will recognise a man of peace. Don't waste time on people if they're not interested in your message.

The clock is ticking, and one day judgment will come (vv. 11–12). Talking about judgment is out of fashion, but Jesus made it more than clear that one day God will call time (see Matthew 13:40–43, 49–50).

3 Peter

Luke 5:1–11

How many times have you been put off by someone saying, 'Oh, we tried that before, but it didn't work'? Before we even start, we are tempted to give up. Contrast this with Simon Peter's response to Jesus in today's passage.

'Put out into deep water and let down your nets for a catch,' says Jesus confidently (v. 4). Peter is a seasoned fisherman, probably still reeling from the disappointment of the previous night's failure, but he's been listening to Jesus for a while now. And there's something almost foolhardy about Peter. He's not a cautious man—he'll take a chance—so he responds, 'Master... because you say so, I will let down the nets' (v. 5).

Do you feel as if you have 'worked hard all night and haven't caught anything'? Is Jesus asking you to try again? What are his instructions to you? Are there some promptings you have never followed up? There is a strong urge throughout the scriptures to 'get on with it'—or 'Just do it', as the sportswear marketing slogan says. See, for example, Exodus 14:15 (the Israelites' escape from the Egyptians), Joshua 3:15–16 (only when the priests stepped into the Jordan river did it stop flowing) and Deuteronomy 32:11 (God, as the parent eagle, pushes the eaglets out of the cosy nest). Don't be afraid to start!

Peter, when he sees Jesus walking on the water, is the one to step out of the boat (Matthew 14:28–29). Yet he has a lot to learn as a disciple. We see his impulsiveness crushed and remoulded ('Get behind me, Satan!' Mark 8:33), but, after his moving reconciliation with Jesus, and another miraculous catch of fish (John 21), it is Peter who plays the lead role in the fledgling church. It is Peter, the 'unschooled' fisherman from Galilee (Acts 4:13), who has the immense privilege of seeing 3000 people come to faith on the day of Pentecost (2:41).

God seems again and again to choose unschooled men and women as his leaders (such as Evan Jones in the Welsh Revival of 1904). Perhaps they are less cautious because they have less to lose. Paul the scholar, by contrast, spent 14 years as an unknown in the desert of Arabia and Damascus (Galatians 1:17—2:1) before he was fully of service to God's mission.

4 Paul

Romans 15:17–22

This is the passage that first inspired me to focus on reaching people who have no prior connection with church (at least 40 per cent in the UK according to the 2007 Tearfund survey *Churchgoing in the UK*). 'It has always been my ambition to preach the gospel where Christ was not known, so that I would not be building on someone else's foundation,' says Paul (v. 20), to explain his delay in reaching the church in Rome. Like the shepherd in Jesus' parable, he would leave the 99 sheep on the hillside and go in search of the one that was lost (Luke 15:3–6).

Similarly, in the UK today, to reach those 'where Christ is not known' means not building on someone else's foundation. That's what is so exciting about the Fresh Expressions movement in the Church of England and the Methodist Church. The vision is not to provide consumerist worship for disaffected Christians but genuinely to go looking for those who are searching spiritually but don't 'get' church. As Jesus put it, 'No one pours new wine into old wineskins' (Mark 2:22).

I may have compared Paul unfavourably with Peter yesterday, but Paul's academic gifting was vital in the pioneering frontiers of mission in the early church. As the Spirit came on the Gentiles, the early church needed to rethink its definition of who was 'in' and who was not (and so the Council of Jerusalem dispensed with circumcision: Acts 15:19–20). We see Paul going even further in Galatians 2. He stops following the law (still beloved to him: Romans 7:12) so that the new community may be based on fewer restrictions. Otherwise it will always seem as if following the law is the best way—a gold standard. Paul 'opposed [Peter] to his face' (Galatians 2:11) because Peter was eating separately from the Gentile Christians. Peter probably didn't intend to make the Gentiles feel 'second class' but, when we've been used to one way of doing things in church for a long time, it is very hard to let go.

As a reader of *Guidelines*, you are probably not an 'unschooled fisherman' like Peter. Paul is my hero. He considered 'everything a loss compared to the surpassing greatness of knowing Christ Jesus my Lord, for whose sake I have lost all things' (Philippians 3:8). Is God calling you to lose some gold standard of 'how to be church' so that the gospel may be preached 'where Christ is not known' today?

5 Mary

Luke 1:26–38

Over my last six years of church planting, Paul has been my hero but Mary has definitely been my role model. Mary is asked to believe that God will do something that sounds totally mad—not unlike Abraham, aged 99, who was called to believe that his children would outnumber the stars in the sky (Genesis 15:5–6).

The birth narratives tell us so much about how God loves to work. First, Mary's best qualification as the Lord's servant was her amazing openness to him (v. 38). Second, there was a time of hidden growth before God's Son entered the world stage. This is often the case with new things that God wants us to bring to birth. We offer a womb for the divine project, where God secretly knits together all the details over time.

Third, birth can often seem poorly planned. Surely God should have planned a smoother entry for his Son than in a draughty last-minute stable? But the early days, as the 'baby' emerges, need to be taken not just a day at a time but often one contraction at a time: 'I am... in the pains of childbirth until Christ is formed in you,' wrote Paul (Galatians 4:19). As J.H. Newman's hymn puts it, 'I do not wish to see the distant scene, one step enough for me.'

Fourth, the baby is soon in danger. Time and again, my experience with pioneering projects has been that the point of birth—going public for the first time—is the most fragile stage. You may well meet anxieties from friends and hostilities from neighbours. Like Jesus' birth, it can seem as if Herod is hell-bent on trying to kill the baby.

Fifth, God works through barrenness. The angel Gabriel announces good news about Mary's cousin Elizabeth: 'she who was said to be barren is in her sixth month' (v. 36). Time and again, God brings life out of barren situations (think of Elizabeth, Hannah, Sarah and Abraham). The children of the promise (Galatians 4:28) are born out of impossibility. This gives us hope.

Sixth, Mary didn't know how it would all work out but she still said 'yes'. In the same way, according to Hebrews 11:8, 'By an act of faith, Abraham said yes to God's call to travel to an unknown place that would become his home. When he left, he had no idea where he was going' (THE MESSAGE)

Is God asking you to say 'yes' to his calling today, even though many things are uncertain about it? Don't expect others to understand your vision. If it's from God, it will come into being: he calls things that are not as if they are.

6 Jesus the pioneer

Hebrews 12:1–13

A seasoned church planter advised me, 'Church planting is easy. It's what gets thrown at it while you're doing it that makes it difficult.' When pioneering in mission, the best tip is this: 'Let us fix our eyes on Jesus' (v. 2). Jesus is the 'pioneer and perfecter of our faith' (NRSV), yet it wasn't easy for him.

First, Jesus himself 'endured the cross' (v. 2). Agony is an intrinsic part of following him: 'We always carry around in our body the death of Jesus' (2 Corinthians 4:10). For Mary, too, saying 'yes' to God was immensely costly: 'a sword will pierce your own soul' (Luke 2:35).

Second, we mustn't 'grow weary and lose heart' (v. 3). Like Abraham, losing faith in God's promise and bearing a child with Hagar (Genesis

16:4), we may settle for a simple human solution. This is the main cause of failure in pioneering mission—nothing dramatic, just that pioneers grow weary and lose heart.

Third, the cross was not the end. In the end, Jesus 'sat down at the right hand of the throne of God' (v. 2). We must never lose sight of where Jesus, our pioneer, is now.

We are being cheered on by a great cloud of witnesses (v. 1). If you feel discouraged, ask God to show you the 'hills full of horses and chariots of fire' (2 Kings 6:17). Also, make a note of what I call 'stones taken out of the Jordan'. In Joshua 4:3, God asked the Israelites to take stones from the riverbed after they had miraculously crossed the Jordan: he knew that, otherwise, they would quickly forget the miracle and start grumbling. So when something special and unexpectedly positive has happened, I note it in my journal.

The Abbé de Tourville, the 19th-century French spiritual writer, puts the task of a pioneer beautifully (*Streams of Grace*, p. 60):

The duty of the pioneer is not easy but it is noble; it is to live in heart and mind with those who are to come. It is for them, rather than for himself, that each in this world works. One could separate mankind pretty clearly into these clearly defined categories: those who live for the past (what good is that?), those who live for the present (very brief and restricted), and those who live for the future (spacious and open, and the satisfaction in doing so increases as time goes on). Think of what little returns Our Lord, the Blessed Virgin and the Apostles gained from their labours… but seen from the future, what enormous results stemmed from their first efforts.

'Therefore, strengthen your weak arms and feeble knees' (v. 12).

Guidelines

At the end of our first week, we take a sabbath moment in our Guidelines. I have the words 'Relax and enjoy' written next to my desk. So much of God's creation was made for simple enjoyment as well as a functional purpose: 'The Lord God made all kinds of trees grow out of the ground—trees that were pleasing to the eye and good for food' (Genesis 2:9).

When moving out in mission, you have your spiritual antennae fully up, but you can't live like this all the time. Just as God found Elijah hiding in the cave, we all need to be refreshed. Elijah experienced God's tender care in his exhaustion, first through the provision of food and water and then through the still small voice of God (1 Kings 19:6–7, 12).

Jesus recognised this pattern, too. In John 21, Peter needed to be refreshed by a tasty fish breakfast on the beach before he could hear God's commission again. Even Jesus noticed that power left him when he performed a miracle (Mark 5:30).

Sabbath moments and sabbath days are essential for restoring the soul. In pioneering mission, there is a danger, as in any responsible job, that we become over-serious. Simon Walker, in *The Undefended Leader* (p. 132), writes, 'See your work as if you were a child helping out their dad. Lose that sense of seriousness and responsibility.'

Relax and enjoy. Be at ease with yourself—because God is. Take time today to consider: what resources you, what relaxes you, and when did you last have fun?

1 Work of prayer

Isaiah 30:15–21

There are many passages that could be chosen on the vital work of prayer, but I have returned to this one again and again. Isaiah's prophecy so visually captures how we will 'have none of it' (v. 15). We fight the enemy in our own strength, rush around on our horses (v. 16), take flight at the slightest opposition (v. 17), and yet the God of compassion longs to give us good things (v. 18). In fact, 'as soon as he hears, he will answer you' (v. 19). As you step forward, 'you will hear a voice behind you, saying, "This is the way; walk in it"' (v. 21).

At the heart of Isaiah's wisdom are the words of verse 15: 'In returning and rest you shall be saved; in quietness and in trust shall be your strength' (NRSV).

Prayer can take many forms. Here are some that have resourced me in particular:

- Prayer as a place of rest in the midst of the demands of ministry (see Mark 6:31). There is a hiddenness about prayer, like the deep roots that resource a tree (Psalm 1:3). The secret of the Christian life is what happens in secret (Matthew 6:6).
- Prayer as a place of trust. Henri Nouwen offers the image of trapeze artists: 'Flyers have to trust their catchers. They can do the most spectacular doubles, triples or quadruples, but what finally makes their performances spectacular are the catchers who are there for them at the right time in the right place... Let's trust the Great Catcher' (*Bread for the Journey*, p. 19).
- Prayer as a weapon (2 Corinthians 10:3–5). Prayer walking round Liverpool has often felt like spreading the 'fragrance' of Christ (2 Corinthians 2:14). John Coles writes about how prayer prepares the ground for sowing seed: 'One of the main reasons why our church in Finchley has enjoyed a prolonged period of relatively fruitful ministry is that a few people were faithfully praying for this church for ten years prior to my arrival' (*New Wine*, Spring 2004).
- Prayer that is ambitious. Jesus tells us, '*Ask* the Lord of the harvest...' (Matthew 9:38) who can do 'immeasurably more than all we ask or imagine' (Ephesians 3:20). We ask such small things of God, and settle for the crumbs of what could be. Why not ask big things of God today? Write a wish list and start praying!
- Prayer to help us 'live by faith, not by sight' (2 Corinthians 5:7). Faith is the envelope for prayer. Jesus said we need faith when we pray (Mark 11:22–24), and he himself assured his disciples, 'The Son... can do only what he sees his Father doing' (John 5:19).

2 Zacchaeus and discipleship

Luke 19:1–10

It is often said that discipleship is the most pressing question in UK church planting today.

As our society becomes less Christianised, we are conscious of the growing gap between our culture and our faith. We sometimes think people need to appreciate that they're sinners before they can accept the gospel.

In fact, I suspect that it's the other way round. Most people think they're not OK and need to hear first of all that God thinks they are OK. This is illustrated brilliantly in the much-loved encounter of Zacchaeus with Jesus. Zacchaeus is already painfully aware that he's an outsider—a 'sinner', as the Pharisees would call him. Perhaps that's why he climbs a tree to see Jesus rather than asking people to allow him to the front of the crowd.

The encounter takes place in four stages. First, Zacchaeus is intrigued by Jesus. Second, Jesus spots him and invites himself round to stay. The crowd are clearly aghast. Fancy accepting someone before they have recognised their sin! But Jesus takes the initiative: it's not that the sin doesn't matter, but that the person is more important. Third, it's when Zacchaeus is in the presence of Jesus, only after he has been welcomed by Jesus, that he is convicted of his sin: 'Look, Lord! Here and now I give half my possessions to the poor' (v. 8). Fourth and finally, Zacchaeus' repentance opens up the way for his full salvation (v. 9). What a privilege to be restored into full standing as a son!

Archbishop John Sentamu puts it pithily: 'Our job is to lead people to Jesus and leave them there.' The temptation is to interpret Jesus for them, and to rush the process. My young son was given a hyacinth that was starting to come into bloom. He thought the flowers looked so pretty that he tried to peel back the ones that were still in bud. It is the same with people I've brought to Jesus: I want to rush them into the full pleasure of knowing him. We can water the plant and put it in sunlight, but the flowers will open in their own time.

Again and again in discipling, I have come back to Jesus' words that it's the Holy Spirit who convicts (John 16:8). This approach does not condone sin: Jesus said, 'Go now and leave your life of sin' (John 8:11), but only after he had restored the adulterous woman into her full status as a daughter of God.

3 Gardening

John 15:1–17

We seem to have lost touch with the organic world of farming in our instant-success, 'click of a mouse' world. Perhaps gardening is now our only link. I have been led back to this passage about God's gardening time and again, especially when the pressure comes (from within myself and from externally) to see 'success'. Here are a few observations.

First, passivity. We are just to *remain in* Jesus, the vine (vv. 4–5). Jesus' parables point to a similar passivity (especially the parable of the growing seed, Mark 4:26–29, where the seed grows even if the sower doesn't bother getting out of bed!). 'Church planting' sounds very active, but Paul—the church planter par excellence—uses passive language too: the church is being built up by God (Ephesians 2:20–22); it is God who makes it grow (1 Corinthians 3:6–7). So don't keep unearthing your seed to see how it is doing. Leave it alone! After anything we do, it's good to leave it in God's hands, as the small boy did with his picnic (John 6:9). Jesus is then able to do some multiplying.

Second, pruning. This is essential for fruitfulness and, so the gardening books tell me, there are particular seasons when pruning is necessary for particular plants. The church planting I was involved in had a clear season of pruning when I found out I was moving away from the city. This was deeply painful, but John 12:24 was very resonant for me at the time: 'Unless a grain of wheat falls to the ground and dies, it remains only a single seed. But if it dies, it produces many seeds.' Do you find yourself or your church in a season of pruning?

Third, patience. Pioneering in mission requires this quality, which is not easily bred in pioneers. I planted sunflowers with my children. We weren't diligent in nurturing and the results were not impressive. Then, two years running, in late September, a flower shot up from a dry shoot that I'd given up watering. Sometimes people will bear fruit long after you've given up watering. 'Part of God's creativity is God's startling patience and willingness to let the work emerge gradually. Impatient people will judge it, dismiss it and walk away. But if we summon up the patience to wait and watch, we may begin to see what God is up to' (Jane Williams, *Approaching Christmas*, p. 44).

Fourth, fruitfulness. For true fruitfulness, keep Jesus central (v. 4)—not your form of church, and not a particular theology. Jesus wants you to bear fruit (v. 16), but be aware that fruitfulness is not the same as 'success'.

4 Failure

Isaiah 49:1–7

Now from questions of fruitfulness to failure—the ever-present spectre for those pioneering in mission. 'But I said, "I have laboured to no purpose; I have spent my strength in vain and for nothing"' (v. 4). This verse has resonated with me countless times, and I suspect that other church planters feel the same: Paul hints at this insecurity in Galatians 2:2.

Yet failure is an inevitable, and necessary, part of trying something new. We have recently moved house and now have a big garden. I am new to gardening. At first I felt overwhelmed by anxiety, in case my new plants failed. Some will fail but, if I didn't plant, there would never be any flowers.

Mother Teresa said, 'God does not ask you to succeed but he does expect you to try.' This is very much the flavour of the Fresh Expressions movement in the Church of England at the moment; as Bishop Graham Cray put it, 'We'd be disappointed if you didn't try.' We will be rewarded for our labour, not our success. In fact, the drive to succeed hampers church planting. Rob Bell writes, 'People who are starting churches... often ask me when I knew it was time to do it. And actually I have a coherent answer: I knew it was time when I no longer cared if it was "successful"' (*Velvet Elvis*, p. 96).

Two anxieties nearly paralysed me at the start of a church plant: will it work, and what will other Christians think? The second anxiety, we will deal with tomorrow.

Over time, my answer to the first anxiety has been to embrace it. It might not work! In his magnificent book on leadership, *The Undefended Leader* (p. 102), Simon Walker recounts the story of Jonathan Edwards, the Olympic triple jumper who had failed in the 1996 Olympics to come anywhere near his records. The 2000 Olympics were his last chance before he retired:

Conventional sporting wisdom would have it that Edwards should have prepared mentally by eliminating the possibility of failure from his mind... But... instead of blocking out failure, he chose to embrace the idea of loss and reflect on what it would actually mean for him never to win an Olympic title... He discovered it was not the threat he had feared it to be. He realised that he could survive such an outcome: he would still know who he was and his identity and worth in God's eyes would still be intact.

Ask yourself today: what are you most afraid of?

5 Testing and temptation

Luke 4:1–13

Jesus' three temptations in the wilderness relate with remarkable resonance to the three biggest temptations I faced as a Pioneer Minister. The Greek can also be translated as 'testings'. The Spirit led Jesus into a time of testing (v. 1); if we are following Jesus, the Spirit will lead us to be tested too.

First, the desire for instant success (v. 3). In the shaky early days, I was actually told, 'It shouldn't be hard; if God's in it, you should get results easily.' Jesus response to the devil harks back to the Sinai desert days (Deuteronomy 8:3), where the people grumbled that God had brought them into the wilderness where there was no bread. The Israelites (like those of us pioneering in mission today) had to learn that it's God who provides the manna—and he delivers just in time, just for that day.

Second, the desire for recognition (v. 5). It is a deeply held human desire to be recognised and acknowledged, but the desire can become corrupted. Tolkien portrays this beautifully in *The Lord of the Rings*, where men are so easily seduced by power that they cannot be trusted to carry the ring—unlike the humble hobbits. Jesus told his disciples, when they were arguing about who was the greatest, 'Whoever wants to become great among you must be your servant' (Mark 10:43), and, in front of little toddlers, he said, 'Anyone who will not receive the kingdom of God like a little child will never enter it' (Mark 10:15). The Carmelites know this. A wise prayer of theirs includes the phrase, 'Grant to us all the humility and trust that will allow you to do great things in us and through us.'

As pioneers, taking risks and trying untried things, we crave the 'well done' from others. Encouragement is good, but this temptation of Jesus reminds us to depend on God alone for the true 'Well done, good and faithful servant!' (Matthew 25:21). Nouwen writes, 'In hiddenness we do not receive human acclamation, admiration, support or encouragement. In hiddenness we have to go to God with our sorrows and joys and trust that God will give us what we most need. In our society we are inclined to avoid hiddenness. We want to be seen and acknowledged' (*Bread for the Journey*, p. 254).

Third, the desire for God on demand (vv. 9–10). Jesus' response, 'Do not put the Lord your God to the test' (v. 12), again harks back to the people of Israel in the desert (Exodus 17:1–7), where they grumbled because there was no water and doubted that God was still with them. They wanted God's miracles on demand, rather trusting in his care.

Which of these three temptations is most alluring to you today?

6 The ascension

Acts 1:1–11

Where did Jesus our pioneer lead us to? Today we read of Jesus' final days on earth. Here are three things to reflect on.

First, Jesus' last words were to a small number of people in a room having a meal together (vv. 4–5). He didn't wow the crowds. (If I'd been recently resurrected, I would certainly have appeared to all the authorities who put me to death!) In fact, there's a sense of disappointment in the air: 'Are you at this time going to restore the kingdom to Israel?' (v. 6). The fragility of this story resonates with Julian of Norwich's picture of creation as a hazelnut: 'I marvelled how it might last, for I thought it might suddenly have fallen to nought for littleness. And I was answered in my understanding: It lasts and ever shall, for God loves it' (*Showing of Love*).

It's a deep human need to feel we've achieved something. Perhaps that is why there are so many grand church buildings. When I handed over the network church earlier this year, there wasn't a grand building project to show for it, just seeds of the kingdom growing among unchurched people scattered across Liverpool. 'The kingdom of God is not coming with things that can be observed... For, in fact, the kingdom of God is among you' (Luke 17:20–21, NRSV).

Second, Jesus wasn't going to bring in his kingdom through political power but through the power of his Holy Spirit. For all the fragility that we sense in pioneering mission, Jesus has left us with his comforter, his advocate, the Holy Spirit himself. The rest of the book of Acts is a thrilling read about how the wild wind of the Holy Spirit blows 'wherever it pleases' (John 3:8) ahead of the apostles, carrying them (sometimes literally: see Acts 8:39) as witnesses to the resurrected Jesus 'to the ends of the earth' (v. 8). When God's Spirit sends us into dark places as his witnesses, we do well to remember that Jesus went to the darkest place, but has won.

Third, Jesus will return (v. 11). He is delaying his return to allow more time for the harvest (2 Peter 3:9), but meanwhile we have all become drowsy and fallen asleep, as Jesus warned in his parable (Matthew 25:5).

As we consider the people and places where we find ourselves today, let us finish where we began, with the compassion of Jesus urging us on in prayer and mission: 'The harvest is plentiful but the workers are few. Ask the Lord of the harvest, therefore, to send out workers into his harvest field' (Matthew 9:37–38).

Guidelines

We began with doom and gloom but we end with hope, with the resurrected Jesus promising his gift of the Holy Spirit, albeit to a straggly, fragile group of apostles. We are their successors today.

As you reflect on these Guidelines in your own context, are there particular people to whom God might be sending you? What big prayers might you pray? What are you most afraid of? Imagine the living Jesus, our pioneer, breaking out from the stained-glass windows into your city, school, workplace and neighbourhood. What does he do and who does he talk to? Which people move his heart with compassion the most? Is he calling you to join him as a worker in the harvest field?

Henri Nouwen's wisdom here has sustained me:

There is a great difference between successfulness and fruitfulness. Success comes from strength, control and respectability. A successful person has the energy to create something, to keep control over its development and to make it available in large quantities. Success brings many rewards and often fame. Fruits, however, come from weakness and vulnerability: community is the fruit

born through shared brokenness, and intimacy is the fruit that grows through touching each other's wounds. Let's remind one another that what brings us true joy is not successfulness but fruitfulness.
BREAD FOR THE JOURNEY, P. 12

RECOMMENDED READING
Henri Nouwen, *Bread for the Journey*, DLT, 1996.
Simon P. Walker, *The Undefended Leader*, Piquant, 2010.
Abbé de Tourville, *Streams of Grace*, Continuum, 2005.
Graham Cray et al., *Mission Shaped Church*, Church House Publishing, 2004.
Steven Croft (ed.), *The Future of the Parish System*, Church House Publishing, 2010.

Tearfund survey:
http://news.bbc.co.uk/1/shared/bsp/hi/pdfs/03_04_07_tearfundchurch.pdf

Deuteronomy 11—22

The book of Deuteronomy is, in many ways, the keystone of the entire Hebrew Bible. Standing at the pinnacle of the Pentateuch (the Torah) and forming the foundation of the history books that follow (the Deuteronomistic history), Deuteronomy lies at the very heart of the Hebrew worldview. Take the pulse of Deuteronomy, and we begin to understand the life that flows through the entirety of Hebrew scripture.

There have been continuing debates in the world of biblical scholarship surrounding the date and authorship of Deuteronomy. Does it stem from true recollections of the speeches of Moses as he addressed the Israelites gathered on the verge of entering the promised land? Did it emerge during the reign of King Josiah (see 2 Kings 22) as he sought to bring about wide-ranging religious and political reforms in the kingdom of Judah? Was it composed to be the theological driving force that would guide the returning Jewish exiles as they sought to rebuild their spiritual and national life?

The compositional history of the book is inevitably obscured by the mists of time, but perhaps the challenges that scholars have faced in pinning it to one particular time and setting also stem from the very nature and success of the book itself, being, as it is, a timeless guide for the life of the people of the Lord. Given its practical spiritual depth and its clarion call to the Lord's people to walk his way and live his life, it should come as no surprise that the book is inseparable from many periods in the history of the Lord's people, from the time of Moses, through the reign of Josiah, to the return from exile in Babylon, and even today. The wisdom of the book of Deuteronomy should lie at the heart of our understanding of what it means to be the people of God—a people so formed by faithful obedience to God that their corporate life effects a missional transformation on the surrounding culture.

All biblical quotations are from the New International Version of the Bible. The studies will be based on a portion of each chapter from 11 to 22, although you may wish to read the whole chapter.

1 Choosing blessing

Deuteronomy 11:16–32

The preaching and teaching of chapters 1—10 now focuses down on the stark choice that is set before the Israelites in 11:26, the choice between blessing and curse. Whether we have in mind the Israelites gathered on the verge of entering the promised land, the people of Judah embarking on the process of the Josianic reforms, the Jewish exiles returning home or, indeed, the journey of Christ's pilgrim people today, the challenge is the same: will God's people go his way (the way of blessing) or will they go the way of all manner of other gods (the way of curse)?

As a permanent physical reminder of the enduring consequences of this choice, the people are instructed in verse 29 to perform a ceremony of blessings and curses once they have entered the land. They are to proclaim blessings from Mount Gerizim and curses from Mount Ebal, the two hills south and north of Shechem, which was later to be the site of a significant covenant renewal ceremony (see Joshua 24). The point being made is vivid and clear: a choice in favour of God and his ways leads to all the blessings of the covenant, while a choice against God leads to the curse of removing oneself from the life of the covenant relationship. The claim is not that the keeping of covenant stipulations leads in a mechanical way to material blessings. Nor is it being claimed that material blessings are a definite sign of righteous living, as is made clear by other writings in the Hebrew scriptures (for example, the book of Job). Rather, the point is that a life of blessing comes from choosing to remain under the care, protection and provision of God, the one revealed personally as YHWH, over against other gods 'which you have not known' (v. 28). The choice is between vain trust in Baal, the Canaanite god who was said to bring rain, fertility and agricultural abundance, and trust in YHWH, the one personally revealed in history as the guardian of all the blessings of creation (v. 17).

The way of life that leads to blessing is highlighted by the text to be the way of deep faith in the Lord and his word. This faith is personally held (v. 18), shared in the family (v. 19) and lived out in the marketplace (v. 20). In other words, blessing comes from faith lived out at all levels, which in turn allows that blessing to spill over into the surrounding culture. Perhaps the challenge for the Church today is to be renewed in its faith in Jesus, at all levels of life, so that the consequent blessings can flood out into the rest of society.

2 One place of worship

Deuteronomy 12:1–14

Whichever horizon we take to be the original setting of Deuteronomy, we can at least be sure of one thing: as is the case in our day, religious pluralism was the context. Rather than happily accepting a multiplicity of religious ideologies, though, the text before us speaks a strong word against the pluralist agenda. In verses 2 and 3, the Israelites are commanded to 'destroy completely' and 'break down' all the paraphernalia of Canaanite worship and to 'wipe out' the names of their gods. Instead, the Israelites are to 'seek the place the Lord your God will choose from among all your tribes to put his Name there for his dwelling' (v. 5). Thus, having removed the presence and power of the 'names' of the Canaanite gods, the Israelites were to fill the cultural arena with the presence and power of the 'Name' of YHWH, the Lord. This agenda is the very opposite of religious pluralism.

The agenda in Deuteronomy 12, however, does not spring from a religious bigotry that seeks to maintain exclusivity. Rather, it seeks to serve the wider aim of universal blessing, which is the goal of the mission of God. The Hebrew scriptures affirm that the one true God was personally and uniquely revealed in YHWH to the people of Israel. The purpose of that revelation, though, was always that the Israelites would be a conduit of blessing to the entire world (Genesis 12:2–3). So, in this wider context, an agenda that seeks to exalt the Name of YHWH and demote the names of any other gods shows a strong commitment to the mission of God to bless and restore the entire creation.

Not only were the Israelites to promote the worship of the name of YHWH over against the names of the Canaanite gods; they were also called to transform the way in which worship was offered (v. 4). Given that the mode of worship reflects the nature of the object of worship, worship was now to reflect the nature of YHWH rather than the gods of Canaan. Sacrificial offerings were to be brought to YHWH's sanctuary rather than to the Canaanite high places (v. 6) because YHWH, not Baal, was to be acknowledged as the creator and provider of material blessings. In order to reflect the exalted moral character of YHWH, worship was now to involve eating and rejoicing in the presence of YHWH (v. 7) in the context of social inclusivity (v. 12), rather than the immoral and exclusive forms associated with Baal worship.

In today's pluralist atmosphere, the challenge for the Church is to boldly and fearlessly worship the name of Jesus in a way that reflects his character in the world, for the sake of the world's blessing.

3 Other gods

Deuteronomy 13

This chapter of Deuteronomy takes its place among those passages of scripture that shock the modern reader. In the space of a few verses, instructions are given concerning the execution of false prophets (v. 5), the stoning to death of apostate family members (vv. 9–10) and the total destruction of towns that have turned to other gods (v. 15). All of this can seem utterly barbaric unless we look beneath the surface to discover the true heartbeat of such a chapter.

The message of the chapter hinges on the importance of Israel's vocation. Having been saved by YHWH from the land of Egypt, the Israelites were called to live in a close covenant relationship with YHWH and model the life of the covenant to other peoples. The false prophet of verses 1–5, even though he comes with impressive signs and wonders, seeks to undermine the very basis of the covenant by leading the people away from a saving relationship with YHWH (v. 5) into the lifeless servitude of idol worship ('gods you have not known', v. 2). The prophet's teaching jettisons the first commandment, seriously jeopardising the covenant relationship and putting the very nature and vocation of Israel at risk. The seemingly harsh treatment of the false prophet in verse 5 should therefore be seen not as barbarism but as an act that seeks to preserve the identity and mission of Israel.

The text is also keenly aware that idolatrous influences can spring up not only in the overtly religious arena (vv. 1–5) but also in the areas of family life (vv. 6–11) and local political leadership (vv. 12–18), contexts that were central to the life of Israel. Important though they were, neither family loyalties nor wider community relationships were to be preserved at the expense of the vital covenant relationship between YHWH and his people. Again, the seemingly harsh instructions of verses 8–10 and 15–17 should be seen as acts of maintaining the covenant rather than religious fanaticism.

Over against the possibility of turning to idols, the text echoes the Shema (compare verse 3 with 6:5) and encourages the people to a close and faithful following of YHWH (v. 4), their personal saving God, who wishes to bless them (v. 17) so that they might be a blessing to other nations.

For the Church today, while we will not seek to revive the legislation of the cultural setting of Deuteronomy 13, this chapter does challenge us to walk faithfully with Jesus and to prophetically expose the modern-day idolatries of our society.

4 Being distinctive

Deuteronomy 14:1–21

The instructions in the previous chapter for dealing with false prophets, idolatrous individuals and apostate communities within Israel may seem far removed from this chapter's instructions on what may and may not be eaten in the Israelite home. Underneath the surface, however, a common principle is at work, namely holiness. As is made clear by the bracketing effect of verses 2 and 21, the various food laws in the intervening verses have their foundation in the distinctive identity of the people of Israel as 'a people holy to the Lord [their] God'. Just as the people were called to maintain their distinctiveness by shunning other gods and obeying YHWH, they were also called to express their holiness through the types of food that they consumed.

Given that the Hebrew scriptures as a whole affirm that all creatures bring glory to God by sharing in the fundamental goodness of his creation, the point being made by this chapter is not that some animals are intrinsically inferior to others. Rather, as indicated by the critical reference to Canaanite mourning rituals associated with Baal worship in verse 1, the chapter's concern is to maintain Israel's distinctiveness over against those practices that characterised Canaanite worship. In verse 3, the Hebrew word translated as 'detestable thing' is the same word that is used in 12:31 to describe Canaanite worship rituals and in 13:14 to describe apostasy in Israel. This indicates that the food laws of verses 3–21 function as regulations for the holiness and distinctiveness of Israel rather than being moral judgments about the intrinsic goodness of the various creatures. Just as Israel was chosen from among many nations to be holy to YHWH, the food laws select some foods from among the many possibilities to be acceptable in the diet of Israel. The food laws were thus a constant daily reminder to the people of Israel of their distinctive calling to be children of YHWH (v. 1), reflecting his nature and likeness to the surrounding nations.

Although the specific food laws of this chapter do not apply to the Church today (due to our very different religious context and the fact that the way is open, in Christ, for Jews and Gentiles to be united), they should cause us to reflect on how we can live a distinctive and holy common life, which blesses the world through reflecting the image of God in Christ.

5 Justice

Deuteronomy 15:1–11

When we compare chapter 13 with this chapter, there may seem to be an incongruous clash between the severity of the instructions on how to treat idolaters within Israel and the warm compassion for the poor that is shown here. Both responses, however, stem from the same underlying heartbeat—the desire to live under the blessing of YHWH through obedience to him. In chapter 13, that obedience takes the form of expelling from within Israel anything that would lead to the worship of other gods. Here, such obedience takes the form of social justice that reflects the very will and heart of YHWH.

Verses 4–6 present an almost eschatological image of the way life is lived under the blessing of YHWH. Here we see that YHWH blesses his people, who then obey him wholeheartedly, with the effect that even richer blessing follows. There is such internal health in this scheme of things that the people are not shackled to other nations by debt (v. 6); nor is poverty an issue among them (v. 4). No legislation is needed in such a blessed situation. The text, however, is well aware that obedience to YHWH will be a continual issue within Israel. The people will be prone to be hard-hearted and tight-fisted (v. 7), and the very laws that have been introduced to remedy their sin may be used to their own advantage (v. 9). The result will be poverty (v. 11).

In order to aim for the vision of verses 4–6, while acknowledging the potential for disobedience, social justice legislation is introduced. In an extension and reapplication of a previous regulation given in Exodus 23:10–11, verses 1–3 provide for the cancellation of remaining loans (and probably also the securities for those loans) in Israel at the end of every seven years. In an echo of the sabbath law outlined in the Ten Commandments (5:12), vulnerable and dependent sections of society are thus protected from slipping into poverty. While loans from trading merchants could be upheld (v. 3), the general mood in Israel was to be one of open-handedness (v. 8) and generosity (v. 10). In this way, Israel would be able to model to other nations a social conscience that reflected the blessings of life lived in obedience to YHWH.

At a time when personal and international debt is such a major factor in poverty, how can the Church model and practise the values of the kingdom, so that the blessed life of fellowship with Jesus can be shown to all?

6 Holy rhythm

Deuteronomy 16:1–17

In what Georg Braulik (former professor of Old Testament studies at the University of Vienna) termed the 'holy rhythm' of Israel's life, we see in this chapter that the covenant relationship between YHWH and his people was to be expressed through the festivals of the agricultural year.

In verses 1–8, the people are given instructions concerning the celebration of the feasts of Passover and Unleavened Bread, which were probably closely associated with each other from very early on in the history of Israel. The association of these two festivals forges a powerful link between celebrating the abundance of the land (there can be no bread without land!) and remembering the saving acts of YHWH in the exodus. By celebrating agricultural abundance in the context of a remembrance of their own salvation history, the people were reminded that it was YHWH, not the gods of Canaan, who was Lord of the harvest. There is a similar link between salvation history and the agricultural year in the celebration of the feast of Tabernacles, described in verses 13–15. During this festival at the end of the grain and grape harvest, the harvesters would live in temporary shelters in the fields as they went about their work. In an echo of the temporary dwellings of the Israelites after the exodus, this was another point of contact between the festivals of the land and the celebration of the saving acts of YHWH.

The agricultural festivals of Israel thus acted as a continuous cycle of remembrance, which formed the people in their identity as YHWH's covenant people. That covenant, however, was not to be understood simply as a one-way flow of blessing from YHWH to the people of Israel. There was also to be an obedient and joyful offering of thanks in return to YHWH, as expressed by the freewill offering of harvest firstfruits at the feast of Weeks (v. 10). In addition, the blessings of the covenant were not to be seen as exclusive gifts. As the agricultural feasts were celebrated, there was to be a deep concern for dependent sections of the population, social inclusivity and justice for those on the fringes of society (vv. 11, 14). The motivation behind all this was the remembrance that the people of Israel themselves had once been marginalised (v. 12).

The 'holy rhythm' of Israel's life formed them as the covenant people of YHWH who were called to be an abundant blessing to the nations around them. What holy rhythms in the life of the Church today can allow us to be a blessing in the world?

Guidelines

As we ponder the book of Deuteronomy, we may have in mind the people of Israel on the verge of entering the promised land, King Josiah carrying out vital spiritual and political reforms, or the Jewish exiles returning home to rebuild their national life. In each case the task is one of mission. Look back over this week's passages of scripture and ponder how they relate to the church's life and mission today. How do the passages in Deuteronomy 11—14 encourage you to live a life of Christ-centred worship in the midst of a pluralist society? How can you live out the life of faith personally, in your family and in public? Looking at Deuteronomy 15, how can you model the kingdom values of justice and compassion? How does Deuteronomy 16 encourage you to build regular times of remembering, thanksgiving and celebration into your life?

1 The king

Deuteronomy 17:14–20

While, in some streams of tradition within the Hebrew scriptures, the king is seen as the human embodiment of YHWH's rule among the people, here a less exalted view of kingship is presented. In this section of the book, which deals with leadership in Israel, the judicial system, not the monarchy, is seen as the fundamental means of YHWH's righteous rule among the people (vv. 8–13). Nevertheless, the text regards monarchy as an allowable form of governance, which can be compatible with the understanding of Israel as a theocracy. As long as the desire for a human king does not stem from an attitude that seeks to break the covenant with YHWH, the divine king (see 1 Samuel 8), the text carries no objection to monarchy as a potentially godly mode of governance.

Given Israel's experience of imperialist domination in Egypt (v. 16) and the seductive pressure to conform to the religious and political culture of the surrounding nations (v. 14), however, the text does give crucial guidance on the character of godly kingship. Unlike the standard picture of kingship in the ancient Near East, the king in Israel was neither to amass great military power (v. 16) nor to acquire a large harem and great wealth (v. 17). Instead, he was to be a leader marked by humility (v. 20), faithful obedience to YHWH and his law (vv. 18–19), and a firm rejection of the gods of the other nations (v. 15). In this way, the king was to embody the covenant values that were to be at the core of the life of every Israelite. He was to be the model Israelite whose leadership reflected the life of the covenant to the surrounding nations.

What is offered here is an ideology of leadership that stands in sharp contrast to the world's ways of hunger for power, self-interest and the amassing of personal gain. A vision of servant-kingship is presented that foreshadows the perfect rule of King Jesus himself. In what ways should this text challenge and form our models of leadership, in both the church and the marketplace, so that the character of Christ is reflected to the surrounding culture?

2 The prophet

Deuteronomy 18:9–22

In every age and culture, people have looked beyond themselves to seek wisdom and guidance for the many challenges and questions of life. A crucial issue, though, in this seeking after wisdom, is whether it is done solely on the basis of human initiative or through a desire to receive revelation from God. The text before us is strongly opposed to the former and strongly in favour of the latter. In verses 9–12, all manner of Canaanite methods for seeking wisdom and guidance are presented, and all of them are based on human initiative and design. The text groups them together with the horrendous practice of child sacrifice (v. 10) because seeking enlightenment apart from the revelation of the one true God leads to no less of a disastrous disintegration of life.

It was not to be that way, however, for the people of Israel. They were not to imitate the 'detestable ways' of the Canaanites (v. 9). Rather, they were to seek and receive YHWH's revelation, mediated through his chosen prophet (v. 15). The description of the prophet in verses 15–18 is the hallmark both of the tradition of true prophecy that was to develop in Israel and of a mysterious future individual who was to arise. In both cases, true prophecy is characterised by four features:

• It arises with the initiative of YHWH, not people (v. 15).
• It follows the pattern of Moses himself, who was the intermediary between YHWH and the people (vv. 15, 18).

- It carries a direct message from YHWH (v. 18).
- It comes with the authority of YHWH (v. 19).

True prophecy is thus characterised by clarity and authority, over against the Canaanite practices of verses 9–12, which are, by comparison, an earthbound scrambling in the dark.

While the hallmarks of the prophet, given in verses 15 and 18, were indeed stamped on the tradition of true prophecy in Israel, the book of Deuteronomy itself claims that no individual prophet 'like Moses' ever did arise again in the Old Testament period (34:10). Verses 15 and 18 thus point forward to a future figure who can be identified as Jesus himself, the one who is 'worthy of greater honour than Moses' (Hebrews 3:3). This text poses an important question for the church today. Do we seek the way forward based on human initiative alone, or do we walk in the clear light of the revelation of Jesus in the scriptures?

3 Innocent blood

Deuteronomy 19:1–13

This section of the book has its roots in the sixth commandment, 'You shall not murder' (Exodus 20:13; Deuteronomy 5:17). The law and judicial system presented in Deuteronomy carries a solemn commitment to bring to justice and punish those who commit acts of murder. The book of Deuteronomy is also frequently concerned, however, with the protection of those who are innocent. Today's text therefore seeks to unite these twin commitments to punish the wicked and protect the innocent in the area of law that concerns murder.

In verses 1–4, the people are instructed to set aside three cities of refuge to which a person can flee for safety if they unintentionally kill someone, an example of which is given in verse 5. This stipulation builds on the instructions in Exodus 21:12–14 and follows the practice of Moses himself, who set aside cities for this purpose, east of the Jordan (Deuteronomy 4:41–43). Precise details of how the system was to function are given in Numbers 35:6–34, and the cities are named in Joshua 20 as Kedesh (in the north), Shechem (in the central hill country) and Hebron (in the south). The text in Deuteronomy 19, though, concentrates more on the essentials of the system. The basic law is outlined in verses 1–4, a model illustration of the principle is given in verses 5–7, a possible expansion of the system is allowed for in verses 8–10, and the obvious exception is stated in verses 11–13.

All of this is built upon the fundamental legal and theological principle expressed in verses 10 and 13, which states that the shedding of innocent blood is incompatible with a righteous standing before YHWH under his covenant blessing. The twin implications are that there must be vindication for the innocent victim of a deliberate murder (vv. 11–13), as well as protection for those who accidentally cause someone's death with no malice aforethought (v. 4).

While our methods of ensuring justice have moved on since the time of Deuteronomy, the text emphasises the timeless and vital need for criminal justice systems to protect the innocent and punish the guilty. In what ways can the church influence the practice of justice so that both the compassion and the justice of Christ are embodied by our society?

4 War

Deuteronomy 20

One of the features of 'the new atheism' has been to try to expose what its proponents see as the inhumane nature of the God of the Old Testament. This has been done by pointing to seemingly rather grisly verses in the Old Testament (such as verse 17 taken in isolation), which, it has to be admitted, many Christians find difficult to reconcile with their faith. The popular commentary, however, often fails to see just how radically progressive was the faith and practice of Israel in the context of the ancient Near East.

Over against the sabre-rattling imperial might of the surrounding nations, which had vast armies of horses and chariots (v. 1), Israel was to place its trust firmly in YHWH (vv. 1, 4), the one who brought them out of Egypt after throwing Pharaoh's horses and riders into the sea (Exodus 15:1). This foundation on the person and character of YHWH led to a radically progressive set of values which were to guide Israel's conduct in the theatre of war.

Firstly, Israel was to prioritise the health and life of its own communities above the war effort. In verses 5–7, we see army officers sending troops home rather than allowing them to face the possibility of death in battle, which would have prevented them from enjoying the blessings of the very land they were fighting for, and would have associated their families with the stigma of curse (see 28:30 in the passage describing curses for disobedience). Secondly, Israel was to show a level of restraint that was unheard of in the context of warfare in the ancient Near East. When they marched on a city, they were first to seek negotiations that might lead to peace (v. 10). These negotiations would probably lead to a vassal treaty, which allowed subject labour (v. 11) but strictly banned any of the violations of human rights that were common in warfare at the time (see, for example, Amos 1:3, 6, 13).

If peace was not possible, however, further restraint was to be shown by sparing the lives of women and children and protecting the livestock and other goods (v. 14). A remarkable level of restraint was also to be shown regarding the natural environment during the conduct of war (vv. 19–20). The seemingly harsh treatment of the Canaanite cities (vv. 16–17) is explained by the critical need to preserve the vocation of Israel at all costs (v. 18).

Israel's distinctively progressive conduct in the arena of war was based on the nature and character of YHWH himself. In situations of conflict today, how can the church reflect the distinctive character and will of Jesus Christ?

5 Atonement

Deuteronomy 21:1–9

This chapter deals with the righting of wrongs, or the lessening of their effects, in the context of human distress. In verses 1–9, it is atonement for an unsolved murder that is in view.

These verses powerfully express the seriousness with which the need for atonement was viewed within the theological and moral framework of the time. In the case of an unsolved murder, the case could not simply be filed away with all the other unsolved cases and forgotten. The understanding was that bloodshed defiled the very land that was YHWH's covenant gift to his people, and that the guilt of bloodshed rested on the whole people (v. 8). A serious seeking of atonement was therefore required, which is expressed here through careful handling of the case (v. 2), specific and elaborate ritual (vv. 3–8) and the involvement of key civic and religious representatives (vv. 2–5). The crucial goal was atonement for bloodshed and the purging of guilt (vv. 8–9).

While the form of the ritual described here is easy to understand, the precise significance of the details is intriguing and difficult to pin down. Commentaries tend to offer two main views on the symbolism involved. Firstly, it could be the case that the heifer is seen as a symbolic substitute for the murderer. Atonement is then achieved by the execution of the heifer (v. 4). This is a reasonable view but it does not take account of the details of the precise location in which the heifer is to be executed. It is for this reason that a second possibility has been suggested. Given that the murder itself took place in a remote location (v. 2), the execution of the heifer in a remote valley (v. 4) could represent a symbolic re-enactment of the murder. The washing of hands (v. 6) and the flowing stream (v. 4) would therefore represent the washing away of guilt, which had been symbolically transferred from the murder site to the re-enactment site.

Whatever the precise meaning of the symbolism involved, the understanding would have been that it was the redeeming covenant grace of YHWH (v. 8), not the mechanism of ritual, that brought atonement and the purging of guilt. This redeeming grace was to go on to find its fullest expression in the cross of Jesus Christ.

As we ponder these verses, a number of questions may arise. Have we lost a sense of the sanctity of life? Have we lost a sense that the collective guilt and shame of society needs to be atoned for?

6   Respecting life

Deuteronomy 22:1–12

In many ways, this final passage of our present studies in Deuteronomy can act as a summary of the key thrust of the twelve chapters we have read. It encapsulates the vision of the people of Israel, living a distinctive life based on passionate obedience to YHWH and his law.

The distinctive life described here is one that seeks to respect life itself at every level. In an extension of Exodus 23:4–5, verses 1–4 affirm that respect for human life should be shown through respect for human property, both animate and inanimate. A lost ox or sheep, a donkey that has collapsed through exhaustion or a misplaced cloak should not simply be ignored. The attitude 'It's nothing to do with me' is incompatible with the call to care for and respect the individual.

Respect for life is expressed by verse 5 in terms of the importance of preserving gender distinction. The people of Israel were to have nothing to do with pagan practices (possibly including ritual transvestism) that in any way damaged the image of God in humanity, as expressed by the distinction of male and female (Genesis 1:27). Respect for life is affirmed in verse 8 through the provision of primitive health and safety guidelines. A parapet around a roof on an Israelite home (which was often used for sleeping and entertaining) would protect both the guests and the owner, who might otherwise become guilty of bloodshed as a result of negligence. The intriguing stipulations of verses 6–7 may express respect for life through a concern for the future propagation of life (which would not be possible if the mother was taken: compare 20:19–20).

The call to distinctive living in everyday life is further emphasised by verses 9–11. Verse 9 is possibly a rejection of various farming practices that were employed by some of the surrounding pagan nations, as well as the Canaanites themselves. On the basis of Leviticus 11:1–8, verse 10 instructs the Israelite farmer not to yoke an unclean animal (a donkey) with a clean animal (an ox), again emphasising the need for distinctiveness over against what was acceptable practice in other nations. The strange stipulation in verse 11 may relate to Egyptian mixed-weave cloth or to garments worn by prostitutes. Again, faithful and distinctive living is in view.

Just as the tassels mentioned in verse 12 were to be reminders of Israel's vocation of faithful obedience to YHWH and his law (see Numbers 15:37–41), the church today must remember its calling to distinctive and holy living, including respect for the sanctity of life.

Guidelines

A constant theme in our reflections on this section of Deuteronomy has been the call to live a distinctive life, based on obedience to YHWH, which reflects his character to the world around. Look back at the passages from Deuteronomy 17—22 and observe the ways in which the people of God are called to live distinctively in the areas of leadership, discerning direction, social justice, conflict and respect for the sanctity of life. What areas of your life need to become more distinctively Christian? Ponder what transformation might result if the church today recommitted itself to living distinctively in the way of Jesus. Pray for the Holy Spirit to empower you for your part in that.

FURTHER READING

J.G. McConville, *Deuteronomy* (Apollos Old Testament Commentary Series), IVP, 2002.

M. Schluter and J. Ashcroft (eds.), *Jubilee Manifesto: A Framework, Agenda and Strategy for Christian Social Reform*, IVP, 2005.

Christmas

Each year, on Christmas Eve, I help to facilitate a short service for young families. It is very informal, with guest appearances from myriad local angels and shepherds who join the nativity group at various points. People from the local community love to come, enjoying the twilight atmosphere, the songs, the tiny musicians and the familiar story. Each year, we become aware of God's presence, which seems to highlight first the youth of Mary, then the kindness of Joseph, and then the magical arrival of the magi. Acting out is a way of remembering, and remembering like this perhaps enables us to receive again the good news of God's amazing love. Those outside the church community are often touched by the incarnate gospel.

My prayer is that as you read these well-known scriptures, you will be touched again by the mystery and the drama of the incarnation. Take a moment each day to ask God to speak to your mind and touch your heart. I have included a short exercise in each reflection, which may help.

Christmas can be a difficult time for many of us, perhaps experiencing busyness, loss or stress. The discipline of taking time to be with God in the midst of life's challenges can be just the resource we need, not simply to survive but to thrive. God has come that we might have life.

'Let the heavens rejoice, let the earth be glad... before the Lord, for he comes' (1 Chronicles 16:31, 33).

Quotations are from the New International Version of the Bible.

1 An angel visits

Luke 1:26–38

How can we fully understand the significance of this moment in history, when a young girl says 'yes' to God? It is a fulcrum—the salvation of us all in the balance, as she receives Gabriel's message and responds. It has been said that 'the hinge of history is on the door of a Bethlehem 'stable' (Ralph Sockman); we might as truthfully say that this is the pivotal moment. The angels in heaven hold their breath.

Twice the angel tells Mary that she has found favour with God (vv. 28, 30). God delights in her and has singled her out, and this blessing steadies Mary to be able to listen to the extraordinary pronouncement: she is to bear a son who will be the promised Messiah, and his father is to be God.

How might a young girl process such a sublime message? Gabriel helps Mary to accept the reality of the situation by giving her a companion on this supernatural journey—her relative Elizabeth, who in later life has been enabled to conceive. Mary, then, is not entirely alone, and the kindness of this provision seems to release her response: 'I am the Lord's servant. May it be to me as you have said' (v. 38).

Mary could not have known how those noble and humble words were to inspire Christians through the millennia. Perhaps she was singled out by God because she already lived as the Lord's servant; her heart was open to his bidding day by day. Was this the woman, then, to whom God could entrust so much? But surely nothing could have prepared her for the total surrender required—to be 'overshadowed' by the Spirit of God and to carry his child. She is for ever a heroine of faith because she so beautifully responded to him. She shows us how to walk humbly with our God (Micah 6:8).

The favour of God will engage us too in his plans, his love for others. The favour of God will be costly for us, as for Mary. Read this passage once more, slowly. Notice which phrase touches you; stay with it and allow your thoughts to explore what it is bringing you. Let it lead you into prayer from your heart.

2 Light dawns

Isaiah 9:2–7

Isaiah was writing during the stormy period when the Assyrian empire was expanding ('the oppressor' of verse 4). He predicted exile and destruction for both Israel and Judah, but in this chapter he looks into a future of deliverance and restoration under the righteous rule of the

Messiah—a king descended from David. Mary may have known this prophecy when Gabriel brought her his message 700 years later.

If you read this passage aloud, you can better grasp the power of the vivid imagery: the light dawning as a wonderful symbol of God's loving deliverance (v. 2), the gathering up of military equipment to be burnt, no longer required (v. 5), and the birth of a child, with his promised kingship (v. 6). Notice the contrast between the breaking of the oppressor's 'rod' (v. 4) and the raising up of God's just reign (v. 7).

Isaiah had a confidence in God's purposes: 'O Lord, you are my God; I will exalt you... for in perfect faithfulness you have done marvellous things, things planned long ago' (Isaiah 25:1).

God is the Wonderful Counsellor, who initiates good plans for his people. Jesus, the promised child, grew up to know the Father's plan and walked in it. This is a source of confidence for us today, even as we live among warring nations and a world driven by economic dictates. He reigns (9:7). In contrast to some world powers, with their oppressive regimes, the Mighty God brings life and peace. As Everlasting Father, his unfailing love holds all things together in Christ, with compassion and protection. He is also the Prince of Peace (*shalom*): he has the well-being of us all on his heart. With 'zeal', God will bring into being a restored world: 'If God is for us, who can be against us?' (Romans 8:31). The energy that lit up the stars in space will deliver us.

Take some time to reflect on an image that has touched you in this passage. Allow the power of it to encourage you as you think about its significance for you. Where, in your life, would you like to see God's *shalom*? Where, in the world, would you wish to bring the love of the Father today?

3 God's kingdom

Luke 1:39–56

After the visitation of the angel, we read that Mary 'hurried' to her relative, Elizabeth: I love that human touch, which hints at all that was going on in her. Eugene Peterson, in THE MESSAGE, translates it, 'Mary didn't waste a minute!'

Why did Elizabeth's baby leap in her womb at the sound of Mary's voice? Mary was carrying the presence of God: it was this that released response from the unborn John and then from Elizabeth, when she spoke prophetically (vv. 42–45). Notice that Mary now heard from a human being the same message she had heard from the angel. These were highly charged moments for both women.

Mary's declaration (vv. 46–55) comes to us in the form of a hymn, one of four in these early chapters of Luke, the others being the songs of Zechariah (vv. 68–79), Simeon (2:29–32) and the angels (2:14).

It begins with Mary's worship to God for his extraordinary favour to her; she also recognises her place in salvation history for generations to come (vv. 46–49): 'What God has done for me will never be forgotten' (*THE MESSAGE*). But the Spirit of God then inspires a vision of the kingdom, which has implications for all. God is at the heart of its coming: he demonstrates mercy (vv. 50, 54), might (v. 51), and a heart not for the rich and powerful but for those who, like Mary, are humble. God has a heart, too, for the hungry (v. 53), for those in need.

Of course, this manifesto was to be reiterated in the theology of Jesus—for instance, in the Beatitudes—but also in the life he lived, seeking out the poor. He showed 'might' as he came against disease, corruption and injustice; he raised up those on the margins and challenged the callous 'rich'.

Is this the manifesto for your church? Do we show a 'bias to the poor' in our communities? Mary's hymn continues to challenge us. Perhaps the secret of fulfilling kingdom values lies in understanding God's invitation to experience his mercy. This is a beautiful word, including the sense of undeserved blessing, the touch of God, goodness given. We read that God remembers to be merciful (v. 54); this is his desire.

Open your hands on your lap and allow God to bring whatever 'mercy' you need today. Tell him what you need and, in faith, receive from him. Ask to be filled with the Spirit. Those who come to God to be filled will become those who themselves show mercy, led by the Spirit.

4 Scripture fulfilled

Who Do You Think You Are? is a television programme that captivates viewers as they are given access to the family histories of well-known people. What is compelling is the extraordinary variety in the ancestry, from slave owners to refugees. The types of people in Matthew's genealogy of Jesus Christ reveal the similarly broad scope of those who make up the people of God. It is into this family history that Jesus is born: God had been at work through all these generations; Jesus is connected to what went on before.

Luke's genealogy (3:23–38) traces the line in reverse order back to Adam, and focuses on Mary's lineage; Matthew, who was writing for a Jewish audience, begins with the father of faith, Abraham, and traces the line of Joseph, the legal 'father' of Jesus in Jewish society. It was a common practice to telescope genealogies; Matthew does this to achieve multiples of seven generations, a symbol of completeness.

The writer of this Gospel was concerned to show Jesus as the fulfilment of Jewish history and scripture, hence this historic opening. He goes on to quote the Old Testament, frequently, in order to compel the reader to see Jesus as the promised Messiah. 'Fulfilled' is one of Matthew's favourite words.

Although reading genealogies seems tedious at first, they can become a reminder of a bigger picture: Matthew wants us to remember that history is God's story. These people are not random names on a page, but part of God's loving purposes, spanning millennia. Jesus redeems history from meaninglessness; you and I are part of *his* story. Finally there will be fulfilment in a new heaven and earth: the book of Revelation looks forward to this part of history, as the genealogy looks back.

God took his place in a family tree. What condescension! And what grace that you and I should be placed in this family: 'How great is the love the Father has lavished on us, that we should be called children of God! And that is what we are!' (1 John 3:1).

What does it mean to you to be part of God's purposes? Receive, with gratitude, this truth. As part of God's family, remember that you are loved: 'You are my son/daughter, whom I love' (see Luke 3:22). Spend some moments in his presence, enjoying your place in his love.

5 Joseph dreams

Matthew 1:18–25

Here is the only narrative in the Gospels that tells of Joseph's response to Mary's pregnancy. He comes across as an upright, gracious man (v. 19), even as he faces this predicament—how to divorce his betrothed quietly, so that she might avoid the severe penalty of stoning.

Even as Joseph considers his course of action, God intervenes, with equal graciousness. He is actively involved in Joseph's thoughts and plans, allaying fear through the gift of a dream. God also chooses the baby's name, reminding Joseph whose son this child really is: legally, the father would have the task of naming, and usually the name would be an inherited one. Joseph would know how significant the name was—meaning 'God saves'.

Notice that Matthew is at pains to point out another fulfilment of God's promises (vv. 22–23). In the book of Isaiah (7:14; 8:8, 10), King Ahaz of Judah was given the sign of a baby son, named 'Immanuel', to reassure him that God would be with him in battle to bring victory: 'Devise your strategy, but it will be thwarted; propose your plan, but it will not stand, for God is with us' (8:10). Jesus, fulfilling this word, fought the ultimate battle over sin and death, on our behalf, to give us the victory we could never win for ourselves.

We know little about the man Joseph, except that he was a carpenter (Matthew 13:55). Perhaps, in this solitary work, he prayed and reflected; perhaps he grew a deep interior life. He learned to attend to his dreams. The important dream described in 1:20–21 was followed by several others, which gave warning and direction to Joseph as he took care of his holy child and precious wife. Like Mary, he had learned to listen to and obey the voice of God.

Joseph grew to be a man of gracious character and attentiveness to God. Many of us have lives and occupations that are far from solitary but, whatever our circumstances, God is with us. It is his Spirit who moulds us, heals us and directs us, as he did Joseph, day by day. God's purposes are still being worked out through his people.

Consider this wonderful thing—that God is working to bless his world through you and me. Quietly offer yourself to God with gratitude, that you might hear him, by day or by night, and that you might walk in the good paths he has for you. 'For we are God's workmanship, created in Christ Jesus to do good works, which God prepared in advance for us to do' (Ephesians 2:10).

6 Zechariah's prophecy

Luke 1:67–79

After weeks of silence—the result of the angel Gabriel's rebuke—Zechariah finally speaks. Words spoken out of previous silence often carry weight, and these certainly do, inspired as they are by the Holy Spirit. The arrival of his baby son prompts Zechariah to declare the impending arrival of a redeeming God (v. 68).

The 'horn of salvation' (v. 69) is a reference to the coming of Jesus; the image of an animal's horn denotes strength and initiative, and the whole passage speaks of God's initiative in bringing salvation. This Messiah will rescue his people from oppressive rulers (vv. 71, 74), from sin (v. 77) and from fear (v. 74). He will come to lead his people into holiness (v. 75) and into peace (v. 79)—not the external efficiency of *pax Romana*, Roman peace, but the deep inner peace of mind and heart that issues from a healed relationship with God and transformed living: 'the knowledge of salvation' (v. 77).

As Zechariah looks at his son, he honours the baby, seeing before him the calling that God has given John—the privilege of preparing hearts and lives to receive forgiveness. He is to be called 'a prophet of the Most High', who points to the Son of the Most High.

Some of the most beautiful words of scripture close the prophecy (vv. 78–79). Who can stop the sun rising? As dawn breaks, its rays fill the skies (a dramatic sight in the Middle East, where this passage was written) with warmth and light. With such majesty and glory Jesus comes, shining light and life into our world, dispelling the 'shadow of death' itself. This, too, is a cosmic moment.

What is the motivation for such a gift? We read that it is 'because of the tender mercy of our God' (v. 78); the Greek means literally the 'bowels' of mercy. This is a graphic word! Perhaps it increases our understanding, our grasp, of the compassion of our God, who has moved heaven to reach out to us with the gift of salvation.

As you pray, you might like to stay with the image of Jesus coming as the rising sun. Allow yourself to be infused by his light and warmth, his presence. Receive again his gift of salvation. Is there something the Spirit wants to say to you?

Guidelines

In the readings this week we have observed heaven and earth touching: there are the angels who visited Mary and Zechariah and there are the dreams that guided Joseph in his decisions. More hidden, perhaps, are the purposes of God being slowly worked out through generations of his people (Matthew's genealogy) and through the prophets (Isaiah). The impact of God on Mary and Zechariah released words of power and truth, which have become part of the liturgy of the church—the Magnificat and the Nunc Dimittis.

The responses of these people were not guaranteed: surrender to God's word was required. Mary's obedience was the door through which the Saviour came. Joseph's obedience gave Jesus a father who would protect him as an infant. Zechariah's obedience set aside his son for a unique calling.

We too can decide to follow God's word, God's agenda. Our obedience can open doors, bless others and release God's kingdom. The Spirit of God helps us in this: Mary surely needed divine help to say 'yes'. When God calls, he equips. In a moment's quiet, offer yourself to God, that through you he might be glorified—heaven touching earth.

24–30 December

1 Jesus is born

Luke 2:1–7

'Two frail moments in the life of Jesus richly bless us: the crib and the cross. There was nothing obviously glorious about these two moments.

His birth was in poverty. His death was also in poverty, outside the walls of Jerusalem, an outcast. These two frail moments became glorious.' So writes a contemporary Benedictine, Macrina Wiederkehr.

Joseph's obligation to register in his home town—demanded by the ruling Roman powers—certainly has no ring of glory about it. Yet do you wonder if he understood that his journey was a fulfilment of the ancient promise that the Messiah would be born in Bethlehem, where the great King David had lived? God was at work in the prosaic challenges of Joseph's life.

Through history, the nativity has captured the hearts and imaginations of artists and believers alike. We read that Mary 'wrapped him in cloths and placed him in a manger, because there was no room for them in the inn' (v. 7). I recall a five-year-old's outrage that this should have been where the King of kings might sleep. Her wonderful response as she sang 'Away in a manger' for the first time reminded me of the frailty of Jesus' birth. He was born not with wealthy relatives in Bethlehem but to a vulnerable family who sought shelter with animals, that they might at least have a roof over their heads. The Son of God was laid in a feeding trough.

Macrina Wiederkehr suggests, 'Our own frail moments can become glorious too.' We experience moments of birthing and dying, times of frailty, but in Christ they can be illumined by his presence. Artists have tried to show the glory in the nativity with golden colour and with a halo around the head of the holy child. Because of the incarnation, we too can know this glory, in us and through us, to touch others—even in the frailty that is ours.

God chose to be born in poverty; he chooses to be born in us. In the carol 'O little town of Bethlehem', we read, 'Where meek souls will receive him, still the dear Christ enters in'—and so he does.

Spend some moments in stillness: imagine that stable and 'see' Jesus in his newborn frailty, lying in the manger. God has come to us. Stay with him and become aware of your response. Express what is in your heart. Allow Jesus to fill you afresh with his love.

2 Shepherds and angels

Luke 2:8–20

Luke was the only non-Jew among the Gospel writers. Perhaps he knew what it was to feel like an outsider in an elitist religious culture: there were so many reasons why you might not be included, whether because of your family, your race or your customs. Luke's Gospel, throughout, brings the message that with God there are no outsiders. He noticed that Jesus included those considered 'outside' by the religious establishment—women, Samaritans, the poor, the sick, and common labourers.

This is what the shepherds were; they tended the flocks kept for temple sacrifices. They may never have been to the temple but God came to them, by sending an angel who carried with him the glory of God. God shone his light and his favour on these hardworking men on the night shift. Moreover, the message the angel brought was one of inclusion: 'good news... for all the people' (v. 10). God's love is for everyone.

With the wonderful message came a response from heaven as the sky filled with praise. Notice how, when the shepherds had visited the Saviour who had been born nearby, they too were caught up in praise (v. 20). The goodness of God touches our whole being and elicits worship. You might like to consider this element in the lives of Mary, Elizabeth, Zechariah and Simeon, too.

These untaught men became the first evangelists: they 'spread the word concerning what had been told them about this child' (v. 17). They could not contain themselves but had to pass on to others this encounter with Jesus, the promised Saviour.

We read that Mary 'treasured up all these things and pondered them in her heart' (v. 19). No doubt the shepherds told her how they had come to be at the stable; it would have been a wonderful encouragement to hear that heaven was rejoicing at the birth. She was also, perhaps, assimilating the truth that God is at home with the lowly and humble of heart (as she had said herself in her Magnificat). Being mother to Jesus was the greatest spiritual lesson.

Take a few moments: ponder, like Mary, these events. Notice what has spoken to you today. Allow your heart, like the hearts of the shepherds, to respond to God.

3 The magi

Matthew 2:1–12

There is more than an element of mystery surrounding these travellers; magi were probably astrologers, who might therefore have been advisers to kings. Herod certainly took them seriously (vv. 3, 7).

They were Gentiles and possibly came from Persia or southern Arabia; their journey had been initiated by the sighting of a 'star' (some suggest that it might have been a planetary conjunction). In their wisdom tradition, it was important to respond to the signs in the sky, and so it was that they were drawn into God's plans to bless the whole world. Their journeying, their asking (v. 2) and their watching (vv. 2, 9) led them to encounter a king beyond their own wisdom and dreams. Notice their wonderful response to the child Jesus: they bow down, they worship and they offer gifts. They are 'overjoyed' (v. 10) to find the one they have been seeking; something is fulfilled in them.

In contrast to these open-hearted men, notice the threatened and scheming character of Herod (vv. 3–8); we know that he dealt with his irrational fear of others by murdering them—even his wife and three sons. So he held a secret meeting with the magi in order to find out as much as possible about this new enemy, and lied to them to win their confidence (v. 8). He had no intention of bowing in worship!

God's Son was born into a world of contrasts—the seekers and the schemers. God's purposes could not be thwarted, however, and the warning dream protected both Jesus and the magi from death (v. 12). The wise men travelled back, guided not by a star but by a word from God in the night.

Over the door of our church is carved, 'Thy face Lord will I seek'. The psalmist who wrote these words (Psalm 27:8) knew where wisdom and life were to be found and, through their seeking, the magi discovered them too. For us, seeking God might mean putting ourselves out, being courageous, asking and watching. Jesus has been called the 'joy of man's desiring' (you might know the Bach cantata: if not, you can listen to a performance on YouTube) and our beautiful passage today reminds us of this truth.

Spend some time in quiet, letting go of situations and worries. Now, like the magi, be in the presence of Jesus. Let his presence be all you need, and let his joy fill you. Respond in words or in silence.

4 Herod's rage

Matthew 2:13–23

When the magi sought direction from King Herod, they were unaware of the huge risk this would bring to the child Jesus. It provoked a crisis for the holy family. Like so many newborns in our world, Jesus was very vulnerable at this time, but his life was spared because of divine intervention (in the form of a dream) and Joseph's swift and obedient response. Joseph had learnt to trust the dreams God sent him: two more (vv. 19–23) later guided them back to Israel—to Nazareth, a rather obscure town in Galilee.

Herod had thought he was in control of the magi; when they 'outwitted' him (v. 16) he flew into a rage that led to brutality and murder, killing all the young boys in and around Bethlehem. It is salutary to recall that whereas on this occasion Jesus escaped death, there came a moment 30 years later when he submitted to the sin and brutality of his enemies, dying on a cross. The slaughter of the innocent children was a foretaste of Jesus' death but also that of his cousin John, and of the many thousands who have died simply because they were Christians. Indeed, the Church has never known as much persecution as it has in our own times; as I write, the Egyptian Coptic Christians are in the news, protesting at the lack of protection as their churches are destroyed and their people massacred.

The battle between the forces of darkness and the grace of God is here made plain. This is not a cosy moment in the Christmas narratives. It is a reminder that we too are in this battle if we follow Christ. He himself warned his disciples that persecution would be part of the road to glory, but the encouragement here is how God's sovereign purposes were being fulfilled. Matthew points us to the scriptures (vv. 15, 17–18, 23) to show us how ancient prophecies were being enacted; Joseph's dreams illustrate again how God intervenes to rescue his people; and we live in the glorious knowledge that Jesus' death would lead to resurrection and the salvation of us all.

Is there something in this passage today that has caught your attention? Stay with it so that you receive more fully what the word of God has to give you. See where your thoughts take you, and use them as a way into prayer. 'Weeping may remain [or visit] for a night, but rejoicing comes in the morning' (Psalm 30:5).

5 The Word entered history

John 1:1–18

The other Gospels speak more of Jesus' human origins; John here speaks of his divine origin. In using the word *Logos*, familiar to his Greek readers as the rational principle that governs all things), John reaches out into Gentile culture to commend the gospel to all.

In the beginning, John writes, there was communion between the Word and God (v. 1) and also he *was* God—a ringing affirmation of Jesus' deity. Then, at one moment in time, the *Logos* entered history, in order to lead us into this communion with the Father, the source of life.

Jean Vanier, in his book about John's Gospel, draws us to verse 14: 'Here is the heart, the centre, the beginning and end of the gospel… and of history'. 'God is no longer distant or set apart from our world': he lived 'among us', visible and vulnerable (see *Drawn into the Mystery of Jesus through the Gospel of John*, DLT, 2004).

Those who walked with Jesus—John the Baptist (v. 15) and the disciples (v. 16)—testified to the extraordinary blessing that his presence brought. They saw that this incarnate God outshone the law of Moses: grace (or love) and truth poured out through him, bringing them into a place of community both with Jesus and with the Father. To quote Vanier again:

Jesus reveals himself in the Prologue
as the unique Son of the Father.
He alone can witness to who God is
because he knows God intimately,
has seen God,
is with God,

and is in God.
He alone shows us the road to oneness with God.

In the Prologue we find epic themes: creation, light, life, birth, faith, truth, the beginning, and God. It is as if John can hardly find the language to do justice to his subject. Jesus appears as the wonderful climax of the passage: his glory has broken into our world (v. 14). Jesus made his dwelling (literally 'tent') among us so that we might find our home in him.

Read the passage slowly, aloud if you can. Allow the magnificence of John's declaration to strengthen your faith. Be still, and let your silence before this mystery be your prayer and worship.

6 Simeon

Luke 2:21–35

This is a remarkable story in the infant Jesus' life, which brings together the members of the holy family, as they seek to fulfil the legal requirements after the birth of a firstborn son, and a man local to Jerusalem. He was no ordinary man, however: we read that he was righteous and devout (v. 25). Moreover, he was a man of the Spirit, sensing that one day he would see with his own eyes the promised Messiah. Notice that beautiful phrase: 'He was waiting for the consolation of Israel'. The Messiah would surely be the one who would bring comfort, healing and peace to a broken world.

And so the moment came when, in the temple courts, they all met. How did Simeon recognise the Messiah? Perhaps he had spent so much time in God's presence that the ability to discern had grown strongly in him: he recognised God. Simeon took the babe in his arms and poured out his heart in prayer and in praise. His longing was fulfilled and God's promise was delivered. The legacy to Simeon was peace (v. 29) and the legacy to the little family was both reassurance and disturbance. How appropriate that the Son of God should be honoured at this moment in the temple (vv. 29–32); how unsettling for his parents to hear of impending conflict and personal pain (vv. 34–35).

There is also a sense that God had waited for this moment to speak through Simeon. Once again we see the interdependence of a sovereign God and his people. There is extraordinary humility in the heart of God. He also grants to Simeon the privilege of blessing the family (v. 34). Faithfulness in his walk with God has led to a moment of amazing joy and a ministry entrusted to him.

Holding the Christ-child must have been the most holy time of Simeon's life; here was the gift of God to all who would receive him. Waiting for God is always rewarded. In his waiting, Simeon grew in trust and love, so perhaps this is an encouragement for us, too, as we wait for the longings of our heart. The key is to practise the presence of God, rest in his goodness, wait for his timing and remain open to being a blessing as he comes.

Think for a moment about Christ Jesus as the 'consolation of Israel'. Pray for those you know who need to know the healing and comfort of the Saviour.

Guidelines

'God said, "Let there be light," and there was light' (Genesis 1:3). This tremendous moment in creation reverberates through history; scientists are now almost able to capture some of those rays of light in their telescopes.

Isn't there something of this in the coming of Christ, the light of the world (John 1:9)? John's Gospel points us to his existence way back then: 'In the beginning was the Word, and the Word was with God' (1:1). Light creates the possibility of life. Jesus is the source of life. In our readings light has featured gloriously as the angels visited the shepherds, and as a beautiful symbol of God's merciful love (Isaiah 9:2; and Luke 1:78–79), coming to the darkness of our sin and brokenness.

Most of us live in well-lit streets, so the contrast between darkness and light is somewhat lost on us today. The scriptures were written in times when a watchman had to guard the city in the hours after dark for fear of attack. The new day brought relief. And so it is that God sent Jesus to set us free from fear. The new day he ushered in brings healing and hope, forgiveness and a new creation. For that is what we are: 'If anyone is in Christ, he is a new creation; the old has gone, the new has come!' (2 Corinthians 5:17).

'The Lord is my light and my salvation' (Psalm 27:1). Spend some moments resting in the presence of God. He it is who called light into being, and he it is who spoke Jesus into our lives. This is his gift to you—a new day.

The BRF

Magazine

The Managing Editor writes...

The BRF Magazine in this issue focuses mainly on the Advent and Christmas seasons, with contributions from Messy Church team member Jane Leadbetter, Barnabas Children's Ministry team member Martyn Payne and regular *New Daylight* contributor Rachel Boulding.

Martyn reminds us of the importance of listening hard to God for his leading, and Rachel, in the featured extract from her Advent book, also mentions the 'attitude of listening' and explains that we can only catch glimpses of the complexity of God's love for us.

During Advent, we prepare for the coming of Emmanuel, 'God with us'—yet it seems that we still need to search him out for ourselves, looking and listening carefully for signs of his presence. After all, the shepherds and the magi had to go looking for the child, even though they were told of his coming in remarkable ways.

We probably know the Christmas story very well, but many others in our society do not. Children need to hear it afresh—and Martyn Payne encourages us to celebrate the work of the Barnabas Children's Ministry team, who bring the Christian faith to life in schools up and down the country. Christmas shoppers in our town centres may know very little of the true meaning of the season—and Jane Leadbetter's innovative 'sheep trail' sends them off on a search for hidden signs of Jesus' coming among us. So those who do not yet participate in the Christian faith are given ways of seeing and hearing of God's love to us at Christmas time.

The old carol by Phillips Brooks, 'O little town of Bethlehem', says:

How silently, how silently
the wondrous gift is given.
So God imparts to human hearts
the blessings of his heaven.

We hope that BRF can offer ways for you to explore that quiet and wondrous gift in these last few months of the year.

Lisa Cherrett

The Messy Nativity project

Jane Leadbetter

Liverpool 2009: there were robins, snowmen, baubles, penguins and Christmas decorations in the city shops. Santa's Grotto bookings were high and new ways of celebrating the season with the family were everywhere, such as giant snow globes to climb into and have a photo taken, or ice rinks popping up in shopping malls where people could skate with Santa and his elves. There were the inevitable pantomimes and Winterfests advertised in the local paper.

So why was I feeling pricklier than Christmas holly this particular year? Because I couldn't find Jesus anywhere as I shopped for Christmas presents. The feeling of consternation stayed with me for a long time until I knew that I had to have a go at doing something about it, no matter how small.

Before working for BRF, I was the Children's Work Adviser for the Diocese of Liverpool. I enjoyed working in collaboration with many Christian organisations, and this Advent I found myself talking with the Liverpool Mothers' Union. Some of their members recalled the Posada activity, in which nativity sets are passed around the homes of church families during Advent, recreating the journey of Mary and Joseph. I also remembered the knitting patterns for nativity characters in the Diocesan Resources Room.

Liverpool is well known for its trails. In the recent past we have had a hugely successful 'Superlambanana' trail around the city, followed by 'Penguins Go!' Families love hunting for decorated models and trying to complete the trails before their friends. With all of this in mind, I was praying about finding local community activities that could be easily prepared, were lots of fun and would bring Jesus back into Christmas in our cities, towns and villages. So, in 2009, a Messy Nativity project began.

The project began with requests for knitters to find knitting patterns for sheep in particular. The MU was very good at hunting down tried-and-tested patterns and, after also looking on the internet, we prepared a pack of suggested sheep patterns. My own daughter created a large version of a knitted sheep and people all over Merseyside began knitting small and large sheep. My life began to change in most unexpected ways. Sheep appeared on my porch, in my car boot and on my desk, and they came in a variety of shapes and colours. Some even had names. Messy sheep seemed to be loved by all ages.

With the Liverpool MU we started Part One of a three-part project for Advent 2010, encouraging parishes to choose a nativity set to pass around the homes in their community, along with knitted sheep. As each home passed the nativity set on to the next, they kept back a small knitted sheep as a reminder of the story. Ideas for a church service or sheep event were shared to bring the community together to experience the real Christmas story. Some Christingle services focused on the sheep and shepherds.

> *At last we had Jesus back in town!*

Part Two of the Messy Nativity project involved placing slightly larger knitted sheep in stores in Liverpool ONE, the city's major shopping and leisure centre. Remembering the trail culture of Merseyside families, I embarked on creating a sheep trail. I gained permission from retail management to ask twelve shops, including GAP, Debenhams, Waterstone's and John Lewis, if I could place a large knitted sheep inside their store. Each store chose where to place the sheep—on counters, on shelving or on the Christmas tree—and they were decorated with tinsel and Christmas bells. Each store was asked to name their sheep for a competition: we had Berry, Bauble, Angel, Dolly, Frank, Don, Kevin, Sheila, Purl, Bertie, Timmy Time and Horace. I promised I would not ask the shop staff to take on any more work, but alongside each sheep would be a pile of sheep trail leaflets. When families had found all the sheep and completed the front of the leaflet with the names, they could take part in a prize draw during Christmas week. Some of the participating stores offered voucher prizes. The rest of the leaflet contained text of the nativity story to take home. At last we had Jesus back in town!

The shops loved the idea, quickly recognising the trail's potential to increase footfall and create a sense of theatre for shoppers. The trail also captured the imagination of local radio and newspaper reporters, who helped to advertise the project. Afterwards, I found some shops very reluctant to give back their sheep, as they had become part of the fixtures and fittings, and I received requests for an Easter trail. Who would have thought that knitted sheep could become so popular with all ages?

Part Three of the project was nearly scuppered by bad weather—nearly! The idea was that, if Jesus was being introduced into homes in local communities and through the nativity story on the trail leaflets, we needed to dramatise the nativity story in the street to passers-by, to help people of all ages realise that Christmas was all about celebrating the birth of Jesus. For this part of the project, I approached a handful of volunteers and we hunted for suitable scripts and props. At this time I was contacted by a chaplain at the city centre indoor market. Could we put on the drama in the market during Christmas week? Perhaps move around, repeating it, and involving the audience—traders, passers-by and so on? What an exciting challenge! The city centre precinct manager heard about it too and invited us to perform the nativity story on the pavements outside. So we had our authorised venues.

We found a simple script that allowed the addition of Christmas carols after each nativity character had been introduced. I ordered small Christmas tracts to give out, and the MU joined us and gave out copies of their *Families First* magazines. Despite the snowfall, we all managed to turn up and had fun performing and encouraging others to be angels and shepherds. On the Saturday we performed the nativity story in four different locations—and we gave out knitted sheep.

> *It is worth doing something rather than nothing*

Since the completion of the Messy Nativity project 2010, I have been contacted by people from all over the country, asking for sheep knitting patterns and help with organising various parts of the project. Cities, shopping malls, towns and villages, north and south of Liverpool, put on their own versions of the project during Advent 2011.

If you would like to do something similar, see page 146 for details of a book to help you. The project can be easily split into three parts. You may feel God asking you just to do one part of the project, but, whatever you choose, remember that it is worth doing something rather than nothing in our present social climate. You may think that you can't make much impact, but just a few key people can make all the difference. Presenting the best story ever told to people who have never heard it is so important. More and more people are oblivious as to why we celebrate Christmas. I believe we need to go into the streets and community at Christmas, where the people are living their busy and messy lives. Come and join in with the mess!

Jane Leadbetter is a member of the BRF Messy Church team.

Barnabas Children's Ministry

Martyn Payne

To my astonishment, 2012 sees me completing ten years with BRF as part of the Barnabas Children's Ministry team—and what an amazing decade it has been! Our face-to-face work with teachers and children in primary schools has grown hugely since I started. Now, for most of the weeks of any given term, the team is in action every day in at least two schools nationally. This is a cause for great praise to God, who has definitely been inspiring and guiding us each step of the way in answer to your faithful prayers and encouragement as BRF readers. Thank you!

Equally exciting has been the growth of our work with churches. This includes both the incredible national and international enthusiasm for a fresh expression of church for children and families in the shape of Messy Church and the existence of our highly respected website for children's leaders and ministers. Many people regularly turn to it for ideas on how to bring the Bible to life for all ages. Put alongside all this our published resources (which continue to receive positive reviews from all quarters) and we clearly have so much to be thankful for.

I have been privileged to be a small part of this phenomenal growth over my ten years with BRF and I am constantly amazed at how God has led me and has blessed our Barnabas work. I hope you too are excited about what is happening and eager to see where God is leading us next.

Looking back, one of the reasons why Barnabas Children's Ministry continues to be so successful is, I believe, that we have been listening closely to what the Spirit of God is saying to the churches about mission among children and families in particular. There is no doubt that children's work through churches is changing, and these changes often demand that we use new approaches and resources, while holding on to our calling to open up the Bible thoughtfully and creatively, which has been at the core of BRF's vision throughout its 90 years.

Our listening has meant that we have embraced and, we hope, contributed to important influences over this ten-year period, such as insights from Godly Play™ as well as the challenge to present Christian truths attractively and faithfully within an educational setting. Our playful, explorative and interactive approach to the Bible has won many friends among teachers, and this same approach seems to meet with the most success in churches, too. It is a methodology that both respects the spirituality of children and gives them space to make their own discoveries about our faith. A mantra of ours has been simply this: that, as we open up the Bible creatively, we can trust this inspired word and the inspiration of the Holy Spirit to inspire children on their own spiritual journey.

Another way in which the Barnabas Children's Ministry team has been listening to God's Spirit can be seen in our passion for Bible story-telling, which has been just right for this day and age. Live storytelling is back in fashion, particularly for a generation that, I believe, welcomes any break from the ever-present image on a screen. We see children's faces light up when they are invited to hear and become part of a story, in which their imaginations can be set free and, most importantly, they can hear God speaking for themselves. Our writing-free, screen-free and worksheet-free approach to sharing the Bible has so much to commend it. This inclusive and interactive way of exploring the great truths of the Gospel is, I believe, much more likely to take root, and it has become a distinctive hallmark of the way our Barnabas team works.

As we look ahead to the next ten years, however, it is clear that we will need to keep listening to God, to discern where he is leading us. For example, we can already sense that much traditional Sunday group work is in decline and that, in its place, a whole-family approach is needed—as made evident by the growth of Messy Church and our new initiative for supporting faith development during the week in the home environment. Put alongside this the increased interest from many churches in how to make true whole-community worship and learning work well—in a way that offers a truly radical intergenerational template for supporting each other on a shared, all-age spiritual journey—and the next ten years look to be as exciting as the last.

I hope you are as thrilled as I am to see what God is doing through BRF on so many fronts. In fact, I believe that we are being as revolutionary today as our founder was at BRF's beginnings, when his first Bible notes began rolling off the St Matthew's printing press 90 years ago. I am so glad that I have been part of this particular adventure. Please join me in waiting eagerly and praying faithfully for the next instalment.

Martyn Payne is a member of the Barnabas Children's Ministry team, based in the south-east of England.

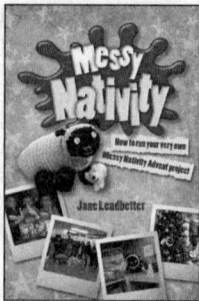

Recommended reading

We may sometimes feel that we're over-familiar with the Gospel stories, especially the Advent and Christmas narratives—so it is always helpful to find new insights and creative ways of learning and teaching these stories. Our 'Recommended reading' in this issue highlights four books that will inspire you to take a fresh look at biblical events and characters, with a special emphasis on ideas for the Advent and Christmas season.

Messy Nativity
How to run your very own Messy Nativity Advent project
Jane Leadbetter

On pages 141–143, Messy Church team member Jane Leadbetter writes about the success of the all-age Messy Nativity Sheep Trail at twelve leading stores in the heart of Liverpool's city centre. The success in Liverpool demonstrates that UK city centres are interested in new and fun ways to attract customers and offer them an experience they will not find online. To help you get involved in your area, BRF is now delighted to announce the publication of *Messy Nativity: How to run your very own Messy Nativity Advent project*. Written by Jane, the book provides all you need to know to set up your own nativity trail and more. Why not order your copy now and join other churches that are bringing Jesus back into Christmas for shoppers across the country?
ISBN 978 0 85746 055 4, pb, 64 pages, £5.99

Messy Christmas Crafts
A treasure trove of Advent, Christmas and Epiphany ideas for Messy Churches
Lucy Moore and Jane Leadbetter

Building on the popularity of *Messy Crafts*, this book extends the range of excitingly messy activities with a particular focus on the Christmas season. There are three complete sessions for Advent, Christmas and Epiphany, together with creative Christmas prayers, global action sug-

gestions, games and competitions, Christmas food crafts and many other ideas to take you on into the New Year.
ISBN 978 0 85746 091 2, pb, 96 pages, £5.99

Jesus: Name Above All Names
32 Bible studies on the person and work of Jesus
Anne Le Tissier

Anne offers straightforward, devotionally based Bible study material on 32 names and titles ascribed to Jesus in scripture. From 'Advocate' to 'Word of God', the studies consider what we can learn about who Jesus is and what he has done for us from the different names and titles. The material also includes questions for response, prayers and suggestions for further Bible reading.

Prepared from articles originally published in *Woman Alive* magazine, which is celebrating its 30th birthday this year.
ISBN 978 0 85746 085 1, pb, 240 pages, £7.99

Walking with Gospel Women
Bible-based meditations
Fiona Stratta

Twenty-five reflective monologues drawing on the voices and stories of women who appear in the Gospel narratives. The approach used is inspired by Ignatian spirituality—imaginatively putting yourself in the context of a particular story (especially one that may already be very familiar) in order to draw out fresh lessons for today. The monologues cover the events of the Gospels, starting with Elizabeth and the annunciation to Mary, and concluding with Mary Magdalene's encounter with the risen Jesus.

The introduction explains how to use the book, including how to facilitate group use.
ISBN 978 0 85746 010 3, pb, 168 pages, £6.99

To order a copy of any of these books, please turn to the order form on page 153, or visit www.brfonline.org.uk.

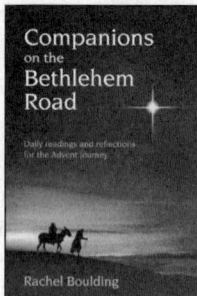

An extract from *Companions on the Bethlehem Road*

This book of daily Bible readings and reflections for Advent and Christmas is based around spiritual insights gleaned from some of the best-loved poets of the past—Eliot, Herbert, Tennyson and Auden, among others. This book is not a literary study of their work but a quest to see what they can tell us about life and faith today. Their poems are quoted in short sections, with suggestions about what they might mean for us now. The following abridged extract is taken from the Introduction to the book.

What poets can show us

I want to suggest that poetry can be enormously helpful in our journey of faith. The poets' finely honed words have much to say to us, right now. They might come from very different ages and backgrounds, but they faced the same questions that we do—about God, human love and the problem of suffering, for example. They have often thought about these questions more deeply than most of us do, and their works endure because the fruit of their reflection still speaks vividly to so many of us…

For it often seems that it is only in poetry that our deepest yearnings can come to the surface. There are so many aspects of God's love for us and ours for him that are hard, if not impossible, to grasp that we can only catch glimpses of part of the picture. The tangential nature of poems—coming at our experience from a particular angle, not feeling they need to record it exhaustively—means that they are ideally placed to convey the complexity, delight and glory of God's care for his creation.

The New Zealand poet James K. Baxter (1926–72) refers to 'an attitude of listening out of which poems may arise… the unheard sound of which poems are translations'. We can make some headway in analysing this attitude but, in the end, it can never be pinned down. God is with us and in us, but also always beyond us. He created us but he doesn't need us; his creation is pure gift.

Poems, which go beyond a merely literal description of the world, hint at this unknowability, this state of reaching towards infinity. As the French poet Paul Valéry (1871–1945) noted, 'A poem is never finished, only abandoned.' Poets are content to explore and deepen the mystery of God, rather than being obsessed with resolving it. So, for example, several poets whom I quote tease out the paradoxes of Jesus' coming from his heavenly kingdom to be born as a defenceless baby—for instance, John Donne (1572–1631) in 'Annunciation' and 'Nativity': 'Immensity cloistered in thy dear womb' (see the readings for 20 December and Christmas Day). They are not studying this paradox as a problem to be explained so much as a mystery to be revelled in...

Advent themes

Advent—the four-and-a-bit weeks before Christmas—is more than just a preparation for the festive season. It is a distinctive time in the Church's year, with its own features, which are a rich blend of different themes. Like Lent, it is a time of penitence, a time to prepare ourselves inwardly for a great festival at its end by reconsidering where we have fallen short. In this respect, it offers a wonderful chance to examine ourselves, to review our lives in a way that we seldom bother to do. We can try to look at ourselves honestly, to probe our sins and repent of them.

> *Poets are content to explore... the mystery of God*

It forms a fascinating interplay with the secular calendar. Advent, the beginning of the Church's year, is when we look both backwards and forwards—just as the secular world does at its New Year, although it concentrates that mood in the few days around 1 January. But, much more than this, the special themes of Advent give it a unique focus, and one that is all too rare for most of us to think about now: death and judgment. The traditional concerns of the four weeks of the season are death, judgment, heaven and hell. This focus also links with the way that, as part of our preparation for the first coming of Jesus at Christmas, churches have traditionally considered its connections with the second coming at the end of time. We look at how the people of God have prepared for this—through the patriarchs and prophets, and on to those directly involved in the events of the nativity: John the Baptist and Mary.

Part of our preparation today involves us in self-examination and penitence, which are sharpened up by our sense of our ultimate end. No matter that most of us manage to put off all thoughts of the end—usually until death becomes an immediate prospect. This season presents a unique opportunity to think about what ultimately matters. It need not be gloomy: the judgment of God offers redemption for the wrongs we have suffered. In the Old Testament, the poor of Israel look forward to it eagerly, as the time when they will be vindicated. Advent Bible readings refer to this redemption specifically: for example, Zechariah's song for his son, John the Baptist, says, 'Blessed be the Lord God of Israel: for he hath visited and redeemed his people' (Luke 1:68: see the reading for Christmas Eve).

During the weeks of Advent, we will be considering these themes but then moving on to ideas about Christmas. Not surprisingly, another part of the point of Advent is to think over Christmas itself, the coming of God into our world—Jesus' becoming one of us and taking on our flesh in the incarnation. The implications of this are staggering, and it should take a lifetime to ponder them. To take just one example, it means that God loves every aspect of our world (as John 3:16 suggests). Jesus entered fully into our humanity; he didn't just visit briefly or dip in his toe. He was not like the Ancient Greek gods who popped down to earth, mainly to cause trouble. Also, we often hear about how incarnational theology should influence our attitude to our planet and to our fellow creatures, human and animal. If God loves the world he has made enough to come and be part of it, we too should cherish it and the other creatures in it. So Advent isn't just about our soul and inner peace: we are only one small part of his whole creation, all under the rule of God into eternity.

About this book

The readings are all drawn from the lectionary, the official pattern of Bible passages set down by the Church for its daily worship. This means that we will always be reading verses alongside other Christians, even if we are on our own. It can be very moving to think that thousands of others are pondering the same parts of scripture, as well as to know that the passages have been specially chosen for this day in the year as part of a carefully thought-out plan to cover the most important aspects of our faith.

The book runs all the way through Advent and the beginning of the Christmas season, right up to the Epiphany on 6 January. Its readings can be used in any year, although the book was first written with Advent 2012 in mind.

To order a copy of this book, please turn to the order form on page 153, or visit www.brfonline.org.uk.

SUPPORTING BRF'S MINISTRY

As a Christian charity, BRF is involved in five distinct yet complementary areas.

- **BRF** (www.brf.org.uk) resources adults for their spiritual journey through Bible reading notes, books, and a programme of quiet days and teaching days. BRF also provides the infrastructure that supports our other four specialist ministries.
- **Foundations21** (www.foundations21.org.uk) provides flexible and innovative ways for individuals and groups to explore their Christian faith and discipleship through a multimedia internet-based resource.
- **Messy Church** (www.messychurch.org.uk), led by Lucy Moore, enables churches all over the UK (and increasingly abroad) to reach children and adults beyond the fringes of the church .
- **Barnabas in Churches** (www.barnabasinchurches.org.uk) helps churches to support, resource and develop their children's ministry with the under-11s more effectively .
- **Barnabas in Schools** (www.barnabasinschools.org.uk) enables primary school children and teachers to explore Christianity creatively and bring the Bible alive within RE and Collective Worship.

At the heart of BRF's ministry is a desire to equip adults and children for Christian living—helping them to read and understand the Bible, to explore prayer and to grow as disciples of Jesus. We need your help to make a real impact on the local church, local schools and the wider community.

- You could support BRF's ministry with a donation or standing order (using the response form overleaf).
- You could consider making a bequest to BRF in your will.
- You could encourage your church to support BRF as part of your church's giving to home mission—perhaps focusing on a specific area of our ministry, or a particular member of our Barnabas team.
- Most important of all, you could support BRF with your prayers.

If you would like to discuss how a specific gift or bequest could be used in the development of our ministry, please phone 01865 319700 or email enquiries@brf.org.uk.

Whatever you can do or give, we thank you for your support.

BRF MINISTRY APPEAL RESPONSE FORM

Name _____

Address _____

_____ Postcode _____

Telephone _____ Email _____

Gift Aid Declaration

❏ I am a UK taxpayer. I want BRF to treat as Gift Aid Donations all donations I make
from 6 April 2000 until I notify you otherwise.

Signature _____ Date _____

❏ I would like to support BRF's ministry with a regular donation by standing order

Standing Order – Banker's Order

To the Manager, Name of Bank/Building Society

Address _____

_____ Postcode _____

Sort Code _____ Account Name _____

Account No _____

Please pay Royal Bank of Scotland plc, Drummonds, 49 Charing Cross,
London SW1A 2DX (Sort Code 16-00-38), for the account of BRF A/C No. 00774151

The sum of _____ pounds on ___/___/___ (insert date) and thereafter the same amount
on the same day each month / same day annually (delete as applic.) until further notice.

Signature _____ Date _____

Single donation

❏ I enclose my cheque/credit card/Switch card details for a donation of
£5 £10 £25 £50 £100 £250 (other) £ _____ to support BRF's ministry

Card no.																

Expires					Security code					Issue no.				

Signature _____ Date _____

Please use my donation for ❏ BRF   ❏ Foundations21   ❏ Messy Church
❏ Barnabas for Children

❏ Please send me information about making a bequest to BRF in my will.

Please detach and send this completed form to: Richard Fisher, BRF,
15 The Chambers, Vineyard, Abingdon OX14 3FE. BRF is a Registered Charity (No.233280)

Please ensure that you complete and send off both sides of this order form.

Please send me the following book(s):

	Quantity	Price	Total
065 3 Companions on the Bethlehem Road (R. Boulding)	_____	£7.99	_____
085 1 Jesus: Name Above All Names (A. Le Tissier)	_____	£7.99	_____
010 3 Walking with Gospel Women (F. Stratta)	_____	£6.99	_____
055 4 Messy Nativity (J. Leadbetter)	_____	£5.99	_____
091 2 Messy Christmas Crafts (L.Moore & J. Leadbetter)	_____	£5.99	_____
063 9 Family Fun for Christmas (J. Butcher)	_____	£4.99	_____

Total cost of books £ _____

Donation £ _____

Postage and packing £ _____

TOTAL £ _____

POSTAGE AND PACKING CHARGES				
order value	UK	Europe	Surface	Air Mail
£7.00 & under	£1.25	£3.00	£3.50	£5.50
£7.01–£30.00	£2.25	£5.50	£6.50	£10.00
Over £30.00	free	prices on request		

**For more information about new books and special offers,
visit www.brfonline.org.uk.**

See over for payment details.

All prices are correct at time of going to press, are subject to the prevailing rate of VAT
and may be subject to change without prior warning.

WAYS TO ORDER BRF RESOURCES

Christian bookshops: All good Christian bookshops stock BRF publications. For your nearest stockist, please contact BRF.

Telephone: The BRF office is open between 09.15 and 17.30.
To place your order, phone 01865 319700; fax 01865 319701.

Web: Visit www.brfonline.org.uk

By post: Please complete the payment details below and send with appropriate payment and completed order form to:

BRF, 15 The Chambers, Vineyard, Abingdon OX14 3FE

Name _____

Address _____

_____ Postcode _____

Telephone _____

Email _____

Total enclosed £ _____ (cheques should be made payable to 'BRF')

Please charge my Visa ❏ Mastercard ❏ Switch card ❏ with £ _____

Card no: ⬚⬚⬚⬚⬚⬚⬚⬚⬚⬚⬚⬚⬚⬚⬚⬚⬚⬚

Expires ⬚⬚⬚⬚ Security code ⬚⬚⬚

Issue no (Switch only) ⬚⬚⬚⬚

Signature (essential if paying by credit/Switch) _____

❏ Please do not send me further information about BRF publications.

BRF is a Registered Charity

BIBLE READING RESOURCES PACK

Thank you for reading BRF Bible reading notes. BRF has been producing a variety of Bible reading notes for over 90 years, helping people all over the UK and the world connect with the Bible on a personal level every day.

Could you help us find other people who would enjoy our notes?

We produce a Bible Reading Resource Pack for church groups to use to encourage regular Bible reading.

This FREE pack contains:

- Samples of all BRF Bible reading notes.
- Our Resources for Personal Bible Reading catalogue, providing all you need to know about our Bible reading notes.
- A ready-to-use church magazine feature about BRF notes.
- Ready-made sermon and all-age service ideas to help your church into the Bible (ideal for Bible Sunday events).
- And much more!

How to order your FREE pack:

- Visit: www.biblereadingnotes.org.uk/request-a-bible-reading-resources-pack/
- Telephone: 01865 319700
- Post: Complete the form below and post to: Bible Reading Resource Pack, BRF, 15 The Chambers, Vineyard, Abingdon, OX14 3FE

Name _____

Address _____

_____

_____ Postcode _____

Telephone _____

Email _____

Please send me _____ Bible Reading Resources Pack(s)

This pack is produced free of charge for all UK addresses but, if you wish to offer a donation towards our costs, this would be appreciated. If you require a pack to be sent outside of the UK, please contact us for details of postage and packing charges. Tel: +44 1865 319700. Thank you.

BRF is a Registered Charity

GUIDELINES INDIVIDUAL SUBSCRIPTIONS

❏ I would like to take out a subscription myself:

Your name _____

Your address _____

_____

_____ Postcode _____

Tel _____ Email _____

Please send *Guidelines* beginning with the January 2013 / May 2013 /
September 2013 issue: (delete as applicable)

(please tick box)	UK	SURFACE	AIR MAIL
GUIDELINE	❏ £15.00	❏ £17.10	❏ £20.25
GUIDELINES 3-year sub	❏ £37.80		
GUIDELINES pdf download	❏ £12.00 (UK and overseas)		

Please complete the payment details below and send with appropriate
payment to: **BRF, 15 The Chambers, Vineyard, Abingdon OX14 3FE**

Total enclosed £ _____ (cheques should be made payable to 'BRF')

Please charge my Visa ❏ Mastercard ❏ Switch card ❏ with £

Card no: ⬜⬜⬜⬜⬜⬜⬜⬜⬜⬜⬜⬜⬜⬜⬜⬜⬜⬜⬜⬜

Expires ⬜⬜⬜⬜ Security code ⬜⬜⬜

Issue no (Switch only) ⬜⬜⬜⬜

Signature (essential if paying by card) _____

To set up a direct debit, please also complete the form on page 159 and send
it to BRF with this form.

GL 0312

GUIDELINES GIFT SUBSCRIPTIONS

❏ I would like to give a gift subscription (please provide both names and addresses:

Your name _____

Your address _____

_____ Postcode _____

Tel _____ Email _____

Gift subscription name _____

Gift subscription address _____

_____ Postcode _____

Gift message (20 words max. or include your own gift card for the recipient)

_____

_____

Please send *Guidelines* beginning with the January 2013 / May 2013 /
September 2013 issue: (delete as applicable)

(please tick box)	UK	SURFACE	AIR MAIL
GUIDELINES	❏ £15.00	❏ £17.10	❏ £20.25
GUIDELINES 3-year sub	❏ £37.80		
GUIDELINES pdf download	❏ £12.00 (UK and overseas)		

Please complete the payment details below and send with appropriate
payment to: **BRF, 15 The Chambers, Vineyard, Abingdon OX14 3FE**

Total enclosed £ _____ (cheques should be made payable to 'BRF')

Please charge my Visa ❏ Mastercard ❏ Switch card ❏ with £

Card no: ▢▢▢▢▢▢▢▢▢▢▢▢▢▢▢▢▢▢▢

Expires ▢▢▢▢ Security code ▢▢▢

Issue no (Switch only) ▢▢▢▢

Signature (essential if paying by card) _____

To set up a direct debit, please also complete the form on page 159 and send
it to BRF with this form.

DIRECT DEBIT PAYMENTS

Now you can pay for your annual subscription to BRF notes using Direct Debit. You need only give your bank details once, and the payment is made automatically every year until you cancel it. If you would like to pay by Direct Debit, please use the form opposite, entering your BRF account number under 'Reference'.

You are fully covered by the Direct Debit Guarantee:

The Direct Debit Guarantee

- This Guarantee is offered by all banks and building societies that accept instructions to pay Direct Debits.
- If there are any changes to the amount, date or frequency of your Direct Debit, The Bible Reading Fellowship will notify you 10 working days in advance of your account being debited or as otherwise agreed. If you request The Bible Reading Fellowship to collect a payment, confirmation of the amount and date will be given to you at the time of the request.
- If an error is made in the payment of your Direct Debit, by The Bible Reading Fellowship or your bank or building society, you are entitled to a full and immediate refund of the amount paid from your bank or building society.
  - – If you receive a refund you are not entitled to, you must pay it back when The Bible Reading Fellowship asks you to.
- You can cancel a Direct Debit at any time by simply contacting your bank or building society. Written confirmation may be required. Please also notify us.

The Bible Reading Fellowship

Instruction to your bank or building society to pay by Direct Debit

DIRECT Debit

Please fill in the whole form using a ballpoint pen and send to The Bible Reading Fellowship, 15 The Chambers, Vineyard, Abingdon OX14 3FE.

Service User Number: | 5 | 5 | 8 | 2 | 2 | 9 |

Name and full postal address of your bank or building society

To: The Manager	Bank/Building Society
Address	
	Postcode

Name(s) of account holder(s)

Branch sort code

| | | | | | |

Bank/Building Society account number

| | | | | | | | | |

Reference

| | | | | | | | |

Instruction to your Bank/Building Society

Please pay The Bible Reading Fellowship Direct Debits from the account detailed in this instruction, subject to the safeguards assured by the Direct Debit Guarantee.
I understand that this instruction may remain with The Bible Reading Fellowship and, if so, details will be passed electronically to my bank/building society.

Signature(s)
Date

Banks and Building Societies may not accept Direct Debit instructions for some types of account.

This page is intentionally left blank.

ND 0310